Illuminate
Publishing

WJEC

AS Media

Studies

S

Study and

Revision Guide

Christine Bell

edited by Barbara Connell

Published in 2012 by Illuminate Publishing Ltd, P.O Box 1160,
Cheltenham, Gloucestershire GL50 9RW

Orders: Please visit www.illuminatepublishing.com
or email sales@illuminatepublishing.com

British Library Cataloguing in Publication Data

A catalogue record for this book is available from the British Library

ISBN 978-1-908682-00-0

Printed by Cambrian Printers, Aberystwyth.

07.15

The publisher's policy is to use papers that are natural, renewable and recyclable
products made from wood grown in sustainable forests. The logging and
manufacturing processes are expected to conform to the environmental regulations
of the country of origin.

Every effort has been made to contact copyright holders of material produced in this
book. Great care has been taken by the authors and publisher to ensure that either
formal permission has been granted for the use of copyright material reproduced, or
that copyright material has been used under the provision of fair-dealing guidelines
in the UK - specifically that it has been used sparingly, solely for the purpose of
criticism and review and has been properly acknowledged. If notified, the publisher
will be pleased to rectify any errors or omissions at the earliest opportunity.

This material has been endorsed by WJEC and offers high quality support for the
delivery of WJEC qualifications. While this material has been through a WJEC quality
assurance process, all responsibility for the content remains with the publisher.

Editor: Geoff Tuttle
Design and layout: Nigel Harriss

Cover photograph: Yuganov Konstantin / Shutterstock.com

Acknowledgements

Sincere thanks to Barbara Connell and Geoff Tuttle for their competent and helpful
editing and exacting input from the beginning.

Jeremy Points of WJEC for his continued support. His encouragement and foresight
enabled this publication to be written.

The team at Illuminate, including Rick, Clare, Geoff and Nigel, for their support, skill
and endless patience.

The authors and publisher wish to thank,

Ashleigh Barbato, Stanwell School, Penarth
Joe Lunec, Heaton Manor School, Newcastle
Toby Freeman, Sussex Downs College

for allowing us to showcase their excellent work.

Dedication

CB – To Nic, Oliver and Lucy.

Contents

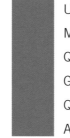

How to use this book

The contents of this study and revision guide are designed to guide you through to success in the WJEC Media Studies AS level examination. This book has been written specifically for the WJEC AS course you are taking and includes useful information to help you to perform well in the examination and the internally assessed unit.

There are notes for the following elements of the AS Media Studies specification:

MS1 – Media Representations and Responses
MS2 – Media Production Processes

Knowledge and understanding

The first part of the book aims to prepare you for the MS1 examination and deals with the three elements of the examination paper:

- textual analysis
- representations
- audience responses.

The **first section** of the book covers the key knowledge required for the MS1 examination. This is your 'Textual Analysis Toolkit'. This is a set of key points and specific media vocabulary that you know you must refer to when analysing a particular media text. Further sections include:

- An overview of the concept of representation and examples of a range of different representations that may appear in different media texts.
- A section on audience considering the ways in which audiences can be defined and categorised; how texts target and appeal to audiences and the ways in which audiences respond to media texts.

You will also find additional support so that you can develop your work:

- Examples of how to analyse a range of media texts including relevant terminology.
- Definitions of key terms and their application to help you in your revision.
- There are Quickfire questions designed to test your knowledge and understanding of the material.
- Examiner tips based on the experience of marking this paper over a period of years and designed to help you to improve your examination technique.
- Grade boosts to illustrate what you need to include in your examination responses to access the higher marks.

- Tasks to encourage you to apply the knowledge and understanding outlined in the guide to the examples you have studied in class.
- We have also highlighted key figures and research to broaden your knowledge and make you aware of the theorists behind the key theories relevant to this subject.
- At the end of each section there is a summary page to help you to structure your revision.

It is important to remember that this is a guide and, although there are examples of annotated texts to help you, it is more important that you gain the knowledge and understanding to allow you to analyse any media texts including your own independently researched examples. It is not the intention that you just use the examples in this guide in your examination responses. These are here to illustrate how knowledge and understanding can be applied effectively – original examples are preferable.

The **second section** of the guide covers the MS2 unit of the specification, which is the internally assessed unit. This considers approaches to research, pre-production and production approaches and tips on how to demonstrate technical and creative competence in your work. There is also support aimed at helping you to write your report and complete your cover sheet. Here you will also find examples of work from 'real' students to give you an idea of what is expected of you at this level.

Exam practice and technique

The **third section** of the book covers the key skills for examination success including the important skill of essay writing and how to structure an examination response. There are also some extracts from sample answers to possible types of questions that may appear in the examination. These are not model answers and you should not attempt to learn them. They offer a guide as to the approach that is required, and the commentary will explain the strengths and weaknesses of the responses. You will be offered advice on how to structure your writing to produce an effective examination response.

Finally, at the end of the book you will find some supplementary material to aid your learning. This includes grids to help note-taking in the examination and a glossary of media terminology.

Most importantly, you should take responsibility for your own learning and not rely on your teachers to give you notes or tell you how to gain the grades that you require. You should look for additional notes to support your study into WJEC Media Studies.

You can look at the WJEC website www.wjec.co.uk. In particular, you need to be aware of the specification. Look for specimen examination papers and mark schemes. You may find past papers useful as well.

MS1: Media Representations and Responses Revision checklist

Tick column 1 when you have completed brief revision notes.
Tick column 2 when you think you have a good grasp of the topic.
Tick column 3 during final revision when you feel you have mastery of the topic.

		1	2	3	Notes
Textual Analysis Toolkit					
p9	Technical codes in moving image				
p12	Technical codes in print texts				
p13	Audio codes				
p13	Visual codes				
p14	Language and mode of address				
p16	Genre				
p17	Narrative				
Print Media					
p20	Magazines				
p22	Print advertisements				
p25	Film posters				
p27	Web pages				
p29	Newspapers				
p32	CD covers				
p34	Computer games covers				
Moving Image Media					
p36	Radio extracts				
p38	Film trailers				
p40	Television extracts				
p42	Music videos				
Representation					
p45	What do we mean by representation?				
p47	Using examples of representation for MS1				
p48	Representations of young people				
p50	Representations of older people				
p51	Representations of events				
p53	Representations of issues				
p55	Representations of women				
p57	Representations of men				
p59	Representations of ethnicity				
p61	Representations of national and regional identity				

		1	2	3
	Audience			
p64	Key points related to an understanding of audiences			
p64	How audiences are positioned			
p65	How audiences may respond to that positioning			
p66	What affects the way in which an audience responds to a media text?			
p67	Audience theories			
p69	How audiences are constructed by media texts			
p69	Audiences categories			
p71	How do media texts target/appeal to audiences?			

MS2: Media Production Processes Coursework checklist

Tick the column when you have understood what is required for each section.

		Notes
p74	**Approaching MS2**	
p77	**Approaching research**	
p80	**Pre-production and production approaches**	
p80	Creating a storyboard	
p83	Creating a script	
p86	Creating print texts	
p88	Creating a moving image	
p90	**Report writing**	
p91	**Cover sheet**	

Representations and responses

MS1 is the examination unit of AS Media Studies. This unit requires you to make links between the media text itself, the representations within the text and the audiences/users that consume it. In your lessons you will explore a range of media texts, focussing on genre, narrative and representation and consider the different ways in which audiences may respond to those texts. Any terms or concepts you do not understand in this introduction will be explained in greater detail in the guide. In this revision guide the key areas you will need to study will be explored including:

Textual analysis

- What is meant by 'genre' and the genre conventions of media texts.
- Narrative construction.
- Technical codes such as camerawork and editing for moving image texts and design elements for print-based texts.
- Language and mode of address.

Representations

- The role of selection, construction and anchorage in creating representations.
- How media texts use representations and the effect those representations may have upon audiences.
- The points of view, messages and values underlying those representations.
- You will be expected to have studied a range of examples of representations in media texts.

Audience responses

- The ways in which audiences can be categorised. For example, by age or cultural background.
- The ways in which the producers of media texts construct audiences and users.
- How audiences and users are positioned.
- The ways in which media texts appeal to and attract audiences.

How will I be assessed?

The MS1 examination is a written examination of two and a half hours. You will be shown some stimulus material which can be taken from a specified list of media areas. If the material is moving image, you will see it three times, the first time you just watch, the second time you may make notes, you will then have ten minutes for further note taking, after which you will see the extract for the third and final time. If the stimulus material is print you will have it with you for the duration of the examination.

Question 1 will require you to analyse the stimulus material. You will be given bullet points to guide you in what you need to write about.

Questions 2 and 3 will be based on audience and representation. Question 2 will be stepped and the first steps will relate to the stimulus material. The last step and question 3 require you to draw on the examples you have studied in class.

For Questions 2c and 3 you must refer to 3 examples from different media forms. This will be explained in more detail under the relevant sections in this guide.

What can I do to help myself?

- Broaden your knowledge and understanding of the media by reading around the subject.
- Read/watch/listen to media texts you are not familiar with or those that are causing discussion in the media generally.
- Read the media sections of newspapers where you will find up-to-date stories and comment about areas of the media.
- Read extracts from text books and articles by media experts and theorists.
- Visit websites dedicated to the subject.

wavebreakmedia ltd/Shutterstock.com

Analysing Media Texts: Textual Analysis Toolkit

Technical codes

In preparation for Question 1 of the MS1 paper it is important that you are able to confidently discuss the technical **codes** of a range of texts and that you are then able to apply that knowledge and understanding across different texts. In order to do this you need a 'Toolkit for Analysis'. This is a set of key points that you know you must refer to when analysing a particular media text. It is also very important that you discuss and analyse the **purpose** and **effect** of the particular technique employed by the text.

Technical codes are one of the ways in which a media text is constructed by the producers of the text. With regard to moving images, including films and television programmes, this is the way in which camera shots, angles and movements are edited together to communicate messages to an audience. In print texts this is the design, layout and key features of the text.

Technical codes in moving image

Camera shots

There are a range of shots that are used to create specific techniques:

Vasilchenko Nikita/Shutterstock.com

Key Terms

Codes = Codes are signs within a media text that give clues to the text's meaning.

Purpose = This is the reason why the technique has been used in the media text. It may be to involve the audience, to develop the narrative or to create tension.

Effect = This is the effect the technical code will have upon the audience. It may make them feel uncomfortable (an extreme close-up), or intrigue them and therefore encourage them to continue watching.

Examiner tip
Analysing technical codes can also help in other areas of the examination paper, for example when discussing how representations are constructed.

- Close-ups are used to create emotion and tension. The close-up on a character's face makes the audience feel involved with the character's feelings. This close-up shot effectively shows the character's feelings and makes the audience feel involved.

- Extreme close-ups, for example a hand on a door handle, or eyes, where information is withheld from the audience, create suspense or highlight the effect of a particular product in an advertisement.

Wouter Tolenaars/Shutterstock.com

Key Term

Production values = These are the features of a media text that show how much it has cost to make. A high budget programme or film is recognisable by its settings, use of stars, more complex editing and soundtrack, for example.

Examiner tip

When you are analysing technical codes consider how they reflect the genre of the media text.

Grade boost

In your examination response, never just name the technical code. Always consider how and why it has been used.

QUICKFIRE

① What other camera shots are there and what are their purpose and effect? Refer to specific examples to illustrate your points

Specific technical codes are used in certain media texts and the audience will expect to see them. They can also be an indication of genre. For example, the medium close-up is also termed the 'news reader shot' as this is how the audience expect the news anchor to be framed on a news programme.

Still taken from YouTube – Fiona Bruce/BBC News at 10 4/10/11

- Long shots are used where more information about the character or the situation is required. Here the audience may be shown the character and part of their surroundings to enhance understanding.

- Establishing shots are rapid ways of advancing the narrative by showing the audience where the action is about to take place. The audience may then have expectations of what will happen next and this enhances their pleasure. For example, the establishing shots of Miami frequently used in *CSI: Miami* suggest the high production values of the programme and give clues to the narrative that will follow according to whether the shot is of a glamorous pool-side location or a seedier, urban one.

Stills taken from YouTube – CBS/CSI: Miami

Camera angles

- A high angle shot with a character as its subject will have the effect of making the character appear vulnerable and insignificant. An aerial or bird's eye view shot is often used in action films and television programmes to film sequences like car chases. It allows the audience to see fully what is happening and also suggests the high **production values** of the programme.

- A low angle shot of a character or object will create a sense of power and dominance. Ground level shots at a very low angle can place the audience in a vulnerable position. This low angle shot of a mystery driver walking towards the camera is taken from the opening sequence of the *BBC Formula One* programme. He is filmed against the light, making him a silhouette and therefore enhancing the enigmatic quality of the image. The low angle shot makes him appear larger than life and powerful. It is a shot used more in film than in sports programmes; he is represented like an action hero.

Still taken from YouTube – BBC Opening titles for F1/ LIQUID TV (2009) directed by Victor Martinez

Editing

- The **editing** of a media text also changes according to the genre – in an action film the expectation is that the editing will be fast paced and the transitions will be cuts to suggest action and speed. In a horror film, for example, the editing may be slower along with the **transitions** in order to build suspense and create enigmas. It is important in analysing texts that their construction through editing is considered. It is also through editing that the narrative is created.

Camera movement

- **Tracking shots** – are used when the camera follows the character or the action. The effect is to make the audience feel involved in the action. If the tracking shot is accompanied by a **hand-held camera**, then the effect of realism and 'being there' is further enhanced. In a reverse track, the camera moves back as the objects come towards the camera. Again, this involves the audience. This shot is used often in hospital dramas where the camera follows the hospital trolley in an emergency or the doors open and the trolley comes towards us. The audience is then caught up in the panic and action.

- **A zoom** – here the camera moves from a long shot in towards the subject. A zoom shot is usually virtually unnoticeable; it should not be intrusive unless that is the desired effect. The zoom to a close-up allows the audience to be involved in the emotion of the character and to more clearly see facial expressions.

- **A panning shot** – in this shot the camera moves horizontally across the scene, imparting information to the audience. It is often used to show location, for example the Miami skyline in *CSI: Miami*. In a whip pan, the camera moves across the scene at high speed causing a blurring effect and suggesting pace and action.

- **In a tilt shot** the camera moves vertically from top to bottom. It can be used to imply mystery when introducing a character by focussing first on the feet and then gradually moving upwards to the face. The audience are then making assumptions about the character in different ways.

Key Terms

Editing = This is the way in which the shots are put together to create a particular effect. Editing can be described in terms of pace and the transitions that are employed.

Transitions = This is the way in which the shots move from one into the other producing a particular effect. Different transitions include cuts which produce a faster paced sequence. Fades and wipes suggest a more controlled and slower section.

Hand-held camera = This is a style of filming whereby a decision has been made not to use the steadicam on the camera but to allow the camera to move freely during filming. This gives a jerky style of filming that suggests realism and makes the audience feel involved in the action.

Examiner tip

If you are shown a moving image clip for the MS1 stimulus material and you are asked to comment on technical codes, you will not have time to mention all of the technical codes you see. Be selective – choose a range of examples and analyse their purpose and effect in the sequence.

Technical codes in print texts

Print texts, like magazines, film posters and CD covers, also use technical codes to transmit meaning. These texts are constructed employing a range of techniques designed to appeal to and attract an audience. These include:

- **Layout and design**. The way in which the print text is constructed is partly through the technical codes of the text. The use of colour, font style and text positioning all contribute to the overall style of the publication. Magazines have a house style and readers recognise this and expect it to be consistent. This may be established through, for example, the font style used for the masthead and the colour codes.

- **Camera shots**. The choice of shot on a print text helps to communicate meaning. A screen shot from a film used on a film poster suggests the narrative and genre of the film. A close-up of the performer on a music industry website contributes to their star persona and attracts their fan base.

- **Lighting.** The way in which the image is lit helps in the construction of messages.

- **Use of colour**. The colours chosen to be incorporated into print texts convey messages about the text's genre and often about the audience who will consume it. Pastel colours employed on a CD suggest a specific type of music. Print-based adverts for fragrances convey messages quickly to their audience by the digitally applied colour washes.

- **Graphics.** Logos and graphical representations appear in many forms on print-based texts. Some CD covers and websites, for example, do not contain images of the band or artist but use more artistic illustrations representing the genre of music. **Graphics** and illustrations are used on the website for *CageThe Elephant.*

- **Post-production techniques.** It is the case in the media today that still images are manipulated and enhanced digitally for an effect. In advertising, eye lashes are extended and skin is made flawless through airbrushing. Models on the front covers of magazines are body brushed to give an unrealistic appearance of perfection.

Key Term

Graphics = This a precise type of design and, in media terms, means the titles and credits in a film or on television, the seemingly hand-drawn, but usually computer-generated illustrations in a games magazine, for example.

Examiner tip

Often, when students are analysing print texts the tendency is to pay less attention to technical codes. Remember that the text has been constructed and the technical codes employed convey meanings to audiences.

quickfire

② How do technical codes construct meanings in print texts? Use specific examples to support your points

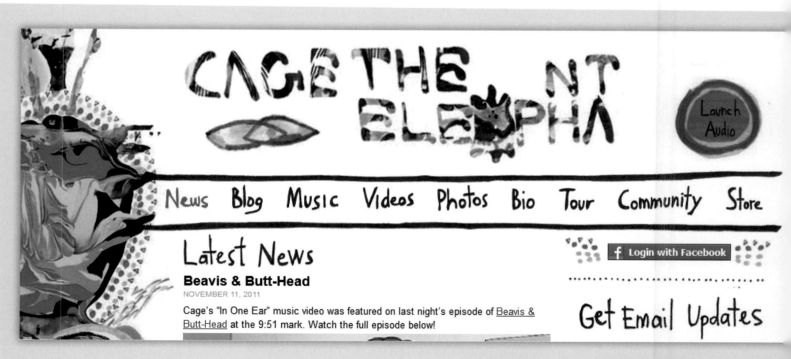

www.cagetheeelephant.com, Sony Music Entertainment

Audio codes

Audio codes are an important way in which the creators of media texts communicate messages. No audio codes are there by chance, they are part of the construction of the text. However, it is invariably the case that students spend less time analysing the audio in favour of the visual elements of the text. It is important that you train yourselves to be able to effectively discuss audio codes, their purpose and effect and to use the correct media terminology to ensure that your analysis is informed and coherent.

Sound in a media text is either **diegetic** or **non-diegetic** and can take the following forms:

- **Dialogue** – this is an important audio code that has the purpose of imparting information to the audience and establishing characters and relationships. The mode of address of the speaker and the specific lexis used can also anchor the text in a particular genre. For example, the ways in which the presenters on *Top Gear* converse establishes a 'pecking order' and creates humour. The technical language they use when reviewing the cars or discussing driving techniques places the programme in its genre.

- **Sound effects** add to the realism of the film or programme and are also an indication of genre and support action codes. For some genres they are enhanced in order to create an effect. For example, in a horror film the sound effects are stereotypical and recognisable – the wind howling and doors creaking. They are made louder post-production in order to build tension and suspense.

- **Music** is obviously an important audio code. The choice of music or the specific song used will convey narrative information to the audience. Music, as with other audio codes, suggests genre. There is an expectation that at a romantic moment in a film, appropriate non-diegetic music will be heard. The audience will **suspend disbelief** as the music adds to the atmosphere. It is often the case that contrapuntal music acts as an action code.

- **Voice-overs** are examples of non-diegetic sound that serve to give information to the audience. For example, the voice-over accompanying a film trailer fills in missing pieces of the narrative for the audience and often establishes the genre through the use of lexis.

Visual codes

One of the ways in which media texts transmit meanings to an audience is through visual codes. Messages are encoded by the producers of the texts and audiences decode these messages. In the section dealing with audience you will see what affects the way in which different audiences interpret and respond to media texts – not all audiences will take away the same messages. Media texts are **polysemic** and contain a range of meanings. Everything we see in a text, whether it is a print text or moving image, will contain meanings. In an MS1 response it is important that you can offer **connotations** and not just a **denotation** of the visual codes contained within the text. The main visual codes are:

- **Clothing** – the clothing worn communicates messages about the person, for example a uniform, a football shirt. Within a media context, clothing can communicate messages quickly to an audience without the need for complex explanation. When a new character enters the frame in, for example, a forensics crime drama and is wearing a white coat and plastic gloves, the audience understands the role of that character and has expectations of their behaviour.

- **Expression** – facial expressions are also ways in which messages are communicated. Combined with close-up shots emotions can be clearly represented in a text and easily interpreted by an audience.

Key Terms

Diegetic sound = This is sound that is part of the mise-en-scene and can be heard by characters in the scene. This may be the heightened sound of cornflakes being crunched in a cereal advert or a gunshot as we see it being fired in a crime drama.

Non-diegetic sound = This is essentially sound that the characters within the frame cannot hear. It is sound that may have been added post-production or has been used to suggest mood and atmosphere.

Suspension of disbelief = This is where the audience are involved in the action and do not question impossible aspects of it; for example, the sound of violins on a deserted beach in a romantic film.

Polysemic = Texts that have more than one meaning contained within them and therefore can be interpreted in different ways by an audience.

Connotation = This is the meaning placed upon the code or sign according to its context. For example, a red rose will have different meanings when on the shirt of a rugby player or in a fragrance advertisement.

Denotation = This is the simple description of what can be seen in the text before meanings are attached it it. For example, the denotation of a red rose is a flower with a strong perfume.

Grade boost

Make sure that you know how to analyse audio by referring to pace, types of instruments, choice of song to match the narrative, purpose and effect. Avoid simplistic descriptions: 'the music was loud'. Consider what made the music loud and why it was important at that point in the text. What effect did it have on the audience?

Key Terms

Symbol = A sign which is understood to refer to something other than itself. A woman wearing a red dress in an advertisement may symbolise that she is passionate or dangerous.

Mise-en-scene = Everything that appears in the frame in, for example, a film or television programme. This includes, iconography, characters and graphics, for example.

Examiner tip

The phrase 'visual codes' may appear as a bullet point for Question 1 of the MS1 paper. Make sure that you understand what is required of you by using this 'Toolkit'. Always consider the impact of the visual codes on the audience.

Grade boost

Avoid simplistic descriptions of visual codes, particularly when discussing colour codes. Always consider the impact, purpose and effect of the visual codes on the audience.

- **Gesture** – gestures are non-verbal communicators and as such, cross language barriers. Characters can convey emotion easily through the code of gesture, for example a shrug, a wave or something more aggressive and offensive. On, for example, music magazine front covers, the gesture and body language of the featured performer may also convey messages about their genre of music.

- **Technique** – the way in which a media text is constructed and presented conveys meaning. For example, the use of black and white photography in an advertising campaign may suggest sophistication and the use of soft focus may carry connotations of romance or emotion.

- **Use of colour** – colours can transmit messages and can be interpreted where they are a key part of a text's construction. For example, in fragrance adverts, they can suggest the type of fragrance being marketed even when the audience cannot smell it. Pastel colours may suggest a light, daytime fragrance whilst darker, rich colours like purples and reds, will convey a sense of a heavier, evening perfume. Advertisements do not have much time to convey meaning so they use colour codes that will be understood by the audience to maximise time.

- **Iconography** – objects, settings and backgrounds within a media text can be analysed for meaning. Some objects within texts take on a significance beyond their literal meaning. The denotation of Big Ben is a clock in London. However, when it appears on *The News at Ten*, it signifies tradition, reliability and London as the centre of news. In this sense it also becomes **symbolic**. Certain media texts are recognisable by their iconography which can place them in a specific genre, for example the setting of the lab and the instruments of a forensic crime drama.

- **Images** – consider the images used within the text. They have been placed within the **mise-en-scene** for a purpose and will communicate messages. For example, the choice of model or celebrity on the front cover of a women's' magazine will give a clue to the target audience of that text. Add to this their code of clothing, gesture and expression and the meaning may become more complex.

- **Graphics** – do not ignore the graphics contained within the text as they too have significance to the meaning. The graphics contained within a film or television trailer, for example the writing on the screen, will convey information about the narrative and the pleasures to be gained from watching the film. In a print text, for example a CD cover, the typography and stylistic features, may give clues to the genre of music and the style of the performer.

Language and mode of address

The ways in which media texts 'speak' to audiences and the language used give clues as to who that audience is and to the genre and purpose of the text. This may refer to the written language of print texts or the spoken word in moving image texts. The language used and the way in which it is used conveys meaning. When analysing language and mode of address consider the following.

Language

Lexis – this means the actual words used by the text. This may pertain to the genre of the text and be recognisable to audiences. Some texts employ subject-specific lexis, for example the front covers of gaming magazines may include lexis that is specific to the world of gaming. Programmes like television hospital dramas will create a sense of realism by employing specific vocabulary linked to the hospital story world. Audiences become familiar with the vocabulary used for particular medical procedures. The effect of this is that the audience who understand the terminology will feel part of the text's community and those who do not will be alienated by the text.

- Language features – certain styles of language are used by certain media texts for a specific purpose:

- Advertisements often use **hyperbole** to make whatever they are selling appear new and exciting.

- Magazines employ **the imperative** to suggest a sense of urgency about what they are suggesting, for example losing weight or getting a six-pack!

- **Ellipsis** is used as an enigma code to encourage the audience to want to buy the magazine and read on.

- The use of slang and **colloquialisms** in, for example, teenage magazines creates an informal relationship between the text and the reader.

- Direct quotations anchor points and suggest realism. These are used on front covers of magazines in cover lines for 'real life' stories.

Mode of address

This is the tone and the written or spoken style of the media text and the way in which it communicates with the target audience. When analysing the mode of address of media texts, consider:

- **Informal mode of address** – some texts, for example magazines aimed at young women, adopt an informal **register**. They use slang, colloquial vocabulary and the personal pronoun to engage their target audience and make them feel as if they are talking directly to them. The audience then feel as if they are part of the seemingly exclusive world of the magazine.

- **Formal mode of address** – other texts, for example quality newspapers, will adopt a more formal style with more complex vocabulary and writing style. This suggests that the target audience are more serious and sophisticated and want more detailed information. News anchors combine a formal mode of address with a serious code of expression, this encourages the audience to trust them and believe what they have to say.

- **Direct mode of address** – this is where the subject of the text communicates directly with the audience. An example would be television presenters like, for example, Bruce Forsyth and Tess Daly in *Strictly Come Dancing*. The effect is to make the audience feel involved with the programme; it is as if they are talking directly to us at home. The anchors of news programmes engage in direct mode of address as they are dealing with serious and important matters. The models and celebrities on the front covers of magazines often look directly out of the magazines, engaging seemingly in direct eye contact with the reader. They draw the audience into the magazine, persuading us to purchase the text.

- **Indirect mode of address** – in many media texts the audience do not expect a direct mode of address. In television programmes and films it would be unusual for the characters to step out of the film world and speak directly to the audience.

Key Terms

Hyperbole = Over-exaggerated language used to create a dramatic effect.

The imperative = These are words or phrases that contain a command or order. They usually end with an exclamation mark, for example 'Get your free gift now!'

Ellipsis = This is where sentences are incomplete and are finished with a set of dots; the words need to be filled in by the reader.

Colloquialism = An informal expression that is more often used in casual conversation than in formal speech or writing.

③ Think of another example of a media text where subject-specific lexis is used. What is the effect upon the audience?

Key Terms

Register = The spoken or written register of a media text is the range and variety of language used within the text. This will change according to the purpose of the text and its target audience.

④ What effect does the mode of address employed have upon an audience?

Grade boost

When analysing media texts for MS1, remember to look closely at the language that is used and consider how it contributes to the impact and attraction of the text.

Key Terms

Hybrid genres = These are media texts that incorporate features of more than one genre. *Strictly Come Dancing* includes features of reality television, game show and an entertainment programme.

Story arc = This is the way in which the narrative progresses from the beginning to the end of the text. A story arc may also cross episodes.

Formulaic structure = This is where the text has a clear structure that is recognisable and rarely changes. For example, the front cover of a glamour magazine has key conventions and the audience has expectations of what will appear on which page throughout the publication.

Examiner tip

The term genre may appear as one of the bullet points for Question 1 of MS1. Make sure that you know and can discuss the key features that establish the genre of a media text.

Examiner tip

Always support the points you make by referring closely to the stimulus material for Question 1.

⑤ What is the repertoire of elements for a genre you have studied?

Genre

One of the bullet points for Question 1 in the MS 1 examination may ask you to comment on the genre of the stimulus material. A genre is the type or category of a media product. Each genre has its own set of conventions or repertoire of elements that are recognisable to audiences. They are what place the text in that particular genre. These key conventions are recognised and understood by audiences by being repeated over a period of time. However, some media texts are **hybrid genres**.

The repertoire of elements can be broken down into key areas:

Narrative

The plot/**story arc** is how the story is told. All media texts convey information through a **formulaic structure**. This may be a linear structure comprising a beginning, middle and end or a non-linear or circular structure. Certain genres have predictable narratives and plot situations within the narrative. For example, the story arc of a soap opera may have several interweaving narrative strands that run through from episode to episode and are focussed on the lives and relationships of a community of characters. A plot situation for a soap opera may be a confrontation between a husband and wife over an affair or an argument in the local pub. This will be covered in more detail on page 17.

Characters

Most genres have a set of recognisable characters, known as stock characters, that help to establish the genre, for example a rebellious teenager in a soap opera. Audiences become used to the character types that appear in certain genres and can predict their behaviour in any given situation. Audiences have expectations as how, for example, James Bond will deal with a particular situation and will be disappointed if he does not conform to type. Stars are also often associated with particular genres and therefore audiences will have an expectation of the role they will play. Actors like Cameron Diaz and Jennifer Aniston, for example, tend to play similar, predictable roles in romantic comedies.

Iconography and setting

CSI: Miami uses the same shots from one series to the next to establish the setting. Objects and props used by the characters may become specific to the genre – the forensic equipment and high-tech labs in *CSI: Miami* distinguish it as an American forensics drama. Clothing and costume is also a rapid way of communicating messages to an audience. The entrance of a character in a white coat with a stethoscope in a hospital drama allows the audience to predict behaviour and the role of that character. This is also true of print texts: the front covers of games magazines may include specific, recognisable iconography that will appeal to a specific audience. On CD covers the iconography may suggest the genre of the music, for example the objects and clothing of a rap artist.

Technical codes

These are very important in establishing genre. Some genres have a particular style of filming and will use certain camera shots and editing. Fast-paced editing with rapid cuts is conventional of action films, whereas slower editing with fades is more conventional of tense dramas. Music industry websites, for example, will often include a range of shots of the performer including close-ups and performance shots in order to establish the music genre. For print texts, audiences have expectations about the technical codes and conventions of the front cover of a lifestyle magazine which may include airbrushing and lighting, for example.

Audio codes

The technical codes may be combined with conventional audio codes, for example the soundtrack that introduces the *BBC News* where the repetitive drum beat rises to a crescendo. Particular sound effects are conventional of certain genres and programmes, for example the sound effect that heralds the arrival of Dr Who's Tardis, which also suggests the action and narratives that will follow. Typical dialogue may be expected in a genre incorporating specific lexis. For example, in a forensics crime drama the audience expect to hear language associated with the subject matter. This enhances the reality.

Narrative

All media texts have a structure or a narrative. The producers of media texts use a variety of techniques to convey the narrative. There are two main types of narrative structures, linear and non-linear or **circular**. Linear narrative was an idea discussed by the theorist Todorov, it conveys the narrative using a chronological structure:

Equilibrium – disruption – conflict – attempt to resolve conflict – climax/confrontation – resolution/return to equilibrium.

Non-linear narrative manipulates time and space and is more challenging for an audience as the narrative moves backwards and forwards. A good example is a crime drama where the beginning may be the discovery of the body, then the audience may be shown the events that led up to the murder, which becomes the middle sequence, and the narrative then moves on to the end where the crime is solved.

Narrative techniques in moving image texts

- **Manipulation of time and space** – narrative shapes a media text in terms of space and time. We, as an audience, are visually transported to America, for example, to watch live sports games. We are also, in programmes like *Match of The Day*, shown action replays and slow motion shots to give us a better understanding of the action. In dramas we are shown long reaction shots to build tension and create empathy with a character.

- **Split screen narratives.** This sometimes occurs in television dramas whereby the screen is split into three or four sections with different mini narratives going on in each of them. For example, in a crime drama this may be: the shot of a body, the killer getting away and the police arriving at the scene.

- **Three strand narratives.** This is a common narrative convention of regular television dramas, for example *Casualty*. At the beginning of the programme three narrative strands will be introduced, for example a continuing problematic hospital relationship, a road accident away from the hospital setting and an incident in the casualty department. As the programme develops, the narratives interweave until the final conclusion. One of the strands will continue into the next episode. This will attract both loyal and one-off viewers.

- **Flexi-narrative**. This is a more complex narrative structure with layers of interweaving narratives. This challenges audiences and keeps them intrigued. The narrative will be ambiguous and characters will develop in their complexity. A good example is the television series *The Killing* which ran for twenty episodes with various suspects and **cliffhangers** before the final surprise denouement.

Key Terms

Circular narrative = This is where the narrative starts at the end and then explores the action up to that point. It is sometimes only at the very end of the film or television programme that the narrative makes sense. For example, in the film *Crash*, the actual crash is at the beginning of the film and then the various narrative strands follow key characters full circle to the same crash at the end of the film.

Cliffhanger = This is a narrative device used at the end of an episode of a drama where the narrative is left unresolved. This encourages the audience to watch the next episode to find out what happened.

Key figure

Tzvetan Todorov is a theorist who researched narrative structures. He suggested that narratives were linear with key points of progression and that narratives involved characters solving a problem ending in a resolution.

Narrative conventions in moving image texts

- **Flashbacks** – are used to give the audience additional information. They may also involve the audience with a character by seeing aspects of their past that contribute to the understanding of the narrative. They are also a way to manipulate time and space within the narrative.

- **Point of view shots** allow the audience to see the action from different perspectives. The camera may **position** the audience as the eyes of the murderer or the victim, or may move between the two in order to build tension.

- **Apparently impossible positions** – this where the camera gives the audience a view of the action from an unusual position, for example in the air or from behind a wall. Audiences tend to accept this view if the narrative itself is believable as this enhances their involvement. A famous example is where the audience is positioned behind the shower wall in *Psycho*. They can see the unsuspecting victim and the shadow of her killer. This clearly enhances the tension of the scene.

The shower scene from Psycho, director Alfred Hitchcock, Paramount Pictures (1960)

Grade boost

Ensure that when you are discussing the narrative of a text you extend your analysis beyond a simple discussion of storyline. Demonstrate your understanding of techniques using appropriate media terminology.

- **Privileged spectator position** – here the camera places the audience in a superior position within the narrative. They are shown aspects of the narrative that other characters cannot see. For example, a close-up showing a character taking a knife out of her pocket. The audience can then anticipate the action that will follow later in the narrative.

- **Enigma codes** are used in both moving image and print texts. In films and television programmes the camera may only show some of the narrative, leaving the audience with unanswered questions. The editing of a film trailer will also use enigmas in the selection of scenes included and voice-overs.

- **Voice-over** – used to move the action on or to fill in missing information. In *Big Brother*, the voice-over establishes what has happened over the last twenty-four hours in order to place the narrative in context. Voice-overs in film trailers explain the story arc to the audience and give us promises of pleasure from the film.

Narrative conventions in print texts

It is not only moving image texts that have narratives. The narrative of any text also refers to its structure and the codes and conventions that are recognisable to audiences. The audience has an expectation of how the narrative of a media text will develop and be conveyed. The narrative of a newspaper involves the front page which tends to be a conventional structure for that particular newspaper, followed by the regular placing of other pages, including the sport on the back page. Film posters convey their narrative through features including a central image, **tag lines** and the name of the film. The narrative techniques used in print texts include:

- **Headlines**. These can convey a detailed and informative narrative in quality papers and may be more dramatic and enigmatic in popular papers where the aim is to attract the attention of the reader.

- **Cover lines** in magazines will give the audience clues to what will appear in the magazine. They may give the start of a story but we need to buy the magazine to get the whole picture. The **jump line** indicates that we need to 'read on'.

- **Images and captions**. The image that appears on the print text can develop the narrative. This may be through the technical codes, the mode of address, the code of clothing or the way in which the audience is positioned by **the look** of the subject. An image without a caption is an open text and the interpretation is up to the audience. Once there is text with the image then the audience will interpret the narrative in a different way and this closes the text. Photographs often capture moments in time and the narrative can be deconstructed to establish meaning.

- **The language** used on a print text will convey messages about the genre of the text and its narrative features. The blurb on the back of a DVD cover is constructed in order to give a taste of the narrative. This may include hyperbole and enigma in order to attract a potential audience.

- **Enigma codes** are a way of holding the interest of the audience. The creator of the text will withhold information and 'tease' the audience so that they will access the whole text in order to find the narrative in its entirety. In print texts enigmas are created through, for example, headlines, tag lines and cover lines.

Key Terms

Tag lines = These are the short slogan-like phrases that sum up a film. They are usually found on film posters and other print promotional material.

Jump line = This appears at the end of a cover line and usually tells the audience which page to turn to in order to read the full story.

The look = This is used to describe the way in which the image on a print text is looking. For example, the mode of address of the model on the front of a glamour magazine may be direct and challenge the audience.

⑥ How can the meaning of an image change according to the words that accompany it?

"A long time ago, in a galaxy far, far away..."
Star Wars (1977)

"Just when you thought it was safe to go back in the water..."
AND
"One good bite deserves another."
Jaws 2 (1978)

"On every street in every city, there's a nobody who dreams of being a somebody."
Taxi Driver (1976)

"In space no one can hear you scream."
Alien (1979)

"Houston, we have a problem."
Apollo 13 (1995)

"The greatest fairy tale never told."
Shrek (2000)

"See our family. And feel better about yours."
The Simpsons Movie (2007)

"He Knows No Fear. He Knows No Danger. He Knows Nothing"
Johnny English (2003)

Key Terms

Sub-genre = Smaller groups within a larger type of media text. Within the magazine genre the sub-genres may include music, gaming and home-improvement magazines.

Lexis = The specific language and vocabulary used to engage the audience. Subject-specific lexis used on the front cover of the magazine will make the reader feel part of the group who belong to the world of that magazine.

Masthead = This is the name of the magazine and, along with the font style, may give clues to the sub-genre, e.g. *Glamour* suggests a fashion/lifestyle magazine.

Sell lines = These are the 'extras' over and above the usual content, e.g. chances to win something.

⑦ How do magazine front covers attract audiences? Give specific examples.

Key figure

Janice Winship is Reader of Media and Film Studies at the University of Sussex. She has engaged in extensive research into the changing representations of girls and women in magazines and the effect that has had on female readers.

Consider how Kerrang! *magazine establishes its sub-genre and attracts an audience*

Magazine front covers

The magazine industry is vast and there are thousands of different titles available across a range of **sub-genres**. It is important that you have the knowledge, understanding and key vocabulary to analyse magazines. Once you have learned how to analyse one magazine you will be able to transfer those skills to magazines from other sub-genres. The front cover of a magazine is a very important selling tool. It is on display and is the first 'taste' of that magazine for the potential consumer.

The aim of a magazine front cover is:

- To attract the target audience.
- To engage the reader by employing an appropriate mode of address and a specific **lexis**.
- To stand out from other magazines of a similar genre.
- To suggest the sub-genre of the magazine through the **masthead**, use of colour, content, etc.
- To engage the attention of the reader through the central image used.
- To establish and reinforce the house style of the magazine.
- To offer reasons for the reader to buy the magazine including **sell lines**.
- To convey an ideology to the target audience, e.g. suggestions of what a 'normal' lifestyle is and to sell the reader that lifestyle.

Kerrang!, *Bauer Consumer Media Ltd*

A range of techniques and strategies are used by magazines to attract and appeal to audiences. One of the most competitive sub-genres is the 'lifestyle' magazine. These magazines for men and women have a high readership and are instrumental in shaping the ideas and views of their audience. They advise their reader on how to live their lives.

Slogan/tag line makes a claim of quality to attract the audience

Masthead suggests high fashion lifestyle

The price is **a sell line** – it may persuade a consumer to buy it instead of the competition.

Central image – uses an 'of the moment' celebrity. Adele is an interesting choice for this magazine as she is not stereotypically glamorous. However, this is not a typical image of this star.

The **discourse and cover lines** of the magazine centre on female narcissism and sex – the magazine constructs the idea of a woman who lives this life.

'Real-life stories' are included to tease the reader into buying the magazine to find out more and makes them feel involved.

Photographer: Simon Emmett, Glamour © The Condé Nast Publications Ltd.

The colour, font style and layout and design conform to a regular pattern and suggest a **house style** – the readers know what to expect from this magazine.

The **mode of address** is chatty and friendly. It speaks directly and informally to the reader 'you' and involves them.

Quick fix problem solving – the magazine suggests it has the answers.

Magazine cover text:
BRITAIN'S No1 WOMEN'S MAGAZINE
GLAMOUR
JULY 2011
www.glamour.com
WOMEN of the YEAR issue
ADELE
On sex and dating celebrities
(what more could you ask for?!)
508 HOT LOOKS
24/7 sunny chic
16 body secrets that work
100% hotness
0% bull
Get what YOU really WANT in BED (so much easier than you thought!)
"I thought celebs were plotting to kill me"
Inside the mind of a schizophrenic
How DO you get to be a magazine editor?
By GLAMOUR's editor

Key Terms

Discourse = The topics and language used by a media text. There are certain topics that would never appear as the discourse of a magazine like *Glamour*. The discourse tends to centre on body image and how to look good.

Cover lines = These suggest the content to the reader and often contain teasers and rhetorical questions.

Mode of address = The way in which a media text 'speaks' to its audience. The mode of address may be formal like a news programme, or informal like this magazine.

House style = This is what makes the magazine recognisable to its readers every issue. The house style is established through the choice of colour, the layout and design, the font style and the general 'look' of the publication.

Grade boost

Never just describe the features of a magazine or any media text. Always explain the purpose and effect of those features.

Print advertisements

Advertising is one of the most powerful media forms and the advertising industry is one of the most lucrative. It is important to be aware of the techniques used by advertisers to attract and appeal to audiences and to promote their products. Advertisers persuade us to buy what we want and desire rather than what we actually need. However, advertising is not solely confined to the selling of consumable products. All sorts of areas of society and companies advertise products – not all of which are for sale. Whatever is being advertised it is important for the advertisers to establish the **brand** and a **brand identity** that the audience will recognise.

Who advertises and why?

- Makers of **consumable products**, e.g. beauty/grooming products – to encourage an audience to buy. This is a very competitive area of the advertising industry.

- Charities – to raise awareness and to encourage donations.

- Government departments, e.g. health – to raise awareness about certain issues, e.g. smoking.

- Organisers of events, e.g. the 2012 Olympics – to boost ticket sales and promote the event to a broad audience.

- Educational establishments – to persuade people to go there for their studies. They produce a prospectus and additional promotional material like flyers.

- The media themselves promote their products through films posters, CD covers, etc.

Key Terms

Brand = That which identifies one company's products from those of another. The branding may be clearly identifiable by a name, logo or some other trademark, for example the font style used by Kellogg's or the Nike swoosh!

Brand identity = The associations the audience makes with brand. This is built up over time. The brand Nike suggests good quality sports clothing that is also fashionable as leisure wear. The high-budget advertising campaigns and sponsorship at world events have helped to reinforce this brand image over time.

Consumable products = These are the products that we use regularly and that need to be replaced. Some audiences are loyal to a particular brand, whereas others may be persuaded to change as a result of successful marketing devices.

QuickFire

⑧ How does the advert featured here differ from adverts for consumable products?

Grade boost

Ensure that you analyse examples of adverts from different types of campaigns to broaden your knowledge of the industry.

Charity and health campaigns have to use different strategies to attract an audience and to convey their message. They have to try to appeal to our emotions by the use of emotive images like the one of this child.

Urgent Stock Appeal

Help us fight for a child's future by donating your unwanted items to this store. Thank you.

Believe in children
Barnardo's

With kind permission of Barnardo's and photographer Mark Stenning

Print advertisements: the Lexus campaign

'A Quiet Revolution' is the 2011 **campaign** launched by Lexus, the car manufacturer, for the world's first hybrid luxury compact car. The campaign uses Kylie Minogue to promote its product. The aim of the new campaign is to target a new audience of younger drivers. Consider the techniques used in the print advertisement.

- The **slogan** suggests being part of something special and 'revolution' is emotive and suggests being at the forefront of something new – the features of this car will appeal to an audience with a social conscience. There is also an **enigma** as the audience is not given all the information about the product.

Lexus/Toyota

- The **colour** scheme is muted and suggests sophistication.

- The **connotations** of the black car suggest sleekness and sophistication.

- The **brand logo** is clearly displayed. The brand is associated with top of the range cars but in the past has marketed to an older audience.

- **Celebrity endorsement** is used to attract the audience. The use of Kylie reinforces the aim of the campaign which is to attract a younger audience. She is attractive and her **code of clothing** suggests sexuality – this will appeal to a male audience. However, she is also a role model for women, which will broaden the audience appeal.

- The **mode of address** is direct and the finger to the lips is a feature of the campaign repeated in other formats. This suggests Kylie is sharing a secret with the audience thus implying the exclusivity of the product.

- There is **iconic representation** so that the audience will recognise the product.

- The **unique selling point** of the advert is the chance to win tickets to Kylie's tour. Lexus is the sponsor of the tour demonstrating cross-format advertising.

Key Terms

Campaign = Run by an advertising agency, this incorporates all the ways in which the product is promoted, e.g. packaging, radio, TV, Internet and print adverts.

Slogan = A catchy phrase that is memorable and thus becomes associated with the product.

Enigma = A mystery contained within the advert that makes the audience curious.

Product endorsement = The use of celebrities, members of the public, experts, etc., to say how good the product is. If the endorser is admired and believable, the audience may be persuaded to buy the product. B&Q use their own staff to add credibility to their products.

Iconic representation = The actual image of the product appears in the advert to show the audience what it looks like, e.g. the image of the perfume bottle is usually featured in fragrance adverts.

Print advertisements: how do adverts work on audiences?

Hard sell = 'In your face' advertising. These adverts are usually short, loud and clearly tell you the price of the product, what it does and where you can get it. The mode of address is direct.

Soft sell = These adverts are much more subtle and attempt to sell a lifestyle rather than just a product. The actual product is not always obvious until the end of the advert.

Appeal = Adverts try to appeal to something within us so that we will buy into the product. They may appeal to our greed or our need for security. Many adverts use the 'herd instinct' appeal by persuading us that everyone else has the product and we will be left behind. Sex appeal is used to sell everything from beauty products to cheese!

Demonstrative action = This is when the audience can see the product being used in the advert, e.g. the hair dye being applied or the floor being cleaned. If we can see it being used, we may believe that it actually works!

⑨ What techniques do print adverts use to promote their products? Include specific examples to illustrate your points.

How do fragrance adverts appeal to an audience?

Inga Ivanova/Shutterstock.com

Print advertisements have to transmit messages very quickly so that they catch your attention as you flick through a magazine or glance at a billboard. All adverts use sophisticated techniques to persuade us to buy into the product, whatever that might be. Reading adverts is a skill you need to master and the following questions will help you to analyse advertisements:

- Language and mode of address – how does the advert 'speak' to its audience? What kinds of words are used and what does that say about the product? Is it a **hard sell** or a **soft sell** advert?

- Narrative – does the advert tell us a story? Is it part of a serial campaign, e.g. BT where we are expected to know the background to the characters, etc.?

- What ideology or messages are conveyed through the advert? Some adverts suggest that purchasing the product will change your life in some way.

- Who is the target audience for the advert and how do you know? How does the advert **appeal** to that audience?

- What are the main appeals used by different adverts?

- How is the product presented to the audience – through **demonstrative action** or as iconic representation?

- Layout and design – how is the print advert constructed? Consider where the images and text are placed and what effect that has.

- Typography and graphics – what can you say about the font styles used or any graphics that appear in the advert? How do they help to persuade the audience?

- Technical codes – consider the camera angles, shots, lighting, editing techniques, e.g. airbrushing, that are used in the advert.

- Endorsement – how does the advert tell the audience how good it is? By using celebrities? Ordinary people? Expert opinions?

- Does the advert use intertextuality so that we make associations between the product and other media forms?

- What roles, models, stereotypes are used in the advert? What associations do they have with what is being sold?

Film posters

Film posters are one of the marketing techniques used by the film industry to promote a new film to an audience. They are a **hook** and are used to persuade an audience to come to see the film. Their aim is to present the key elements of the film to a fleeting audience; an audience who may be walking past and will not necessarily stop and look at the poster in detail. The poster must therefore encapsulate the film in the images and words contained within it. The posters often contain enigmas to encourage the audience to want to come and watch the film in order to discover the answers to the questions posed by the poster. **Teaser campaigns** use this device very effectively. The poster also creates an identity for the film and often includes iconic images that will appear in other marketing material.

The posters for *The Dark Knight* showed the iconic image of The Joker staring directly out at the audience. The images were disconcerting and suggested the darker tone of this film. One of the posters has the tag line 'Why So Serious' with the character seeming to be drawing a smile in blood on a steamy window. Others show him dishevelled and with smudged makeup in the rain. The images are enigmatic and encourage the audience to want to find out more about the character and the narrative.

Key conventions of film posters

Genre indications: the images and **copy** on the poster will usually give a clue to the genre of the film.

- Iconography – this is another clue to the genre of the film. The objects, background, clothing and setting will establish the genre of the film.

- Promise of pleasure – these are the words and phrases that tell the audience what they will experience through watching the film, e.g. fear, laughter, etc.

- Star billing – the positioning of the images or the names of the stars on the poster. Sometimes there is a hierarchy of importance.

- Stars – the stars can also give a clue to the genre – Jennifer Aniston is associated with romantic comedies and Harrison Ford with action/adventure films.

- The tag line – this is the memorable phrase or slogan that becomes associated with the film and appears on the marketing material.

- The image – this will have been carefully chosen and may suggest the narrative of the film and the role of the key characters.

- Language and mode of address – this will be persuasive and often makes use of **hyperbole**.

- Expert criticism – quotes from newspapers, film magazines and reviews suggesting the quality of the film and making it a 'must see'.

Yuganov Konstantin/Shutterstock.com

Key Terms

Hook = This is the element of a media text that catches the attention of the audience and draws them in. On a film poster it may be the image, the tag line or the copy.

Teaser campaign = This is when the film posters are part of a sequence whose aim is to release more information about the film gradually in the run up to the release. The campaign employs enigmas to catch the interest of the audience by withholding information.

Copy = This is the writing on the media text.

Hyperbole = This is over-exaggerated language used to enhance the attraction of the text and the experience.

10 **Why are genre indications and stars important to the marketing of a film?**

Grade boost

Remember to analyse the film poster as one element of the overall campaign to promote the film. Analyse the key features, highlighting their purpose and effect. Avoid just describing what you can see.

When analysing a film poster in the MS1 examination or creating a poster as part of a coursework submission, it is important to be aware of the key conventions and to be able to use relevant media vocabulary specific to the format.

The poster has a narrative conveyed through the film title and the central image. It is enigmatic and encourages the audience to want to know more.

Key Terms

Mark of quality = This is usually the film logo, the director's name or references to other successful films made by this director. These are included to convince the audience that this new film is a quality product.

Expert witnesses = This is where the poster includes quotes from experts who the audience will trust, e.g. *Empire Magazine*, Mark Kermode, etc. If they give the film positive reviews and we trust them, we are more likely to go and see it. However, quotes are often taken out of context or edited to make the comment seem more positive. Remember, this is not the whole review!

Examiner tip

Remember that although the focus of this section is 'Textual Analysis', this example can also be used to effectively discuss audience and representation for the other questions on the paper.

Examiner tip

When you are faced with a text like this to analyse in the examination, make sure that you do not just tell the examiner what you can see. Look for the more complex messages and codes that are contained within the text and consider how it tries to appeal to its audience.

Mark of quality: references to other successful films of a similar genre.

The mode of address is direct and challenging and subverts the connotations of the title.

The quotes make comparisons with films that would attract a similar audience.

The film title is a hook and, combined with the image, gives the audience expectations of the film.

Expert witnesses are used in the quotes to suggest the film is unmissable.

Courtesy of Universal Studios Licensing LLC

The code of gesture is provocative and challenges what the audience might expect of 'bridesmaids' thus suggesting the comedy element.

The 'save the date' suggests that everyone will be going to see the film and thus encourages the audience not to feel left out.

The use of star ratings suggests the quality of the film.

The code of clothing is used to give the characters individual personalities that we assume will be explored as part of the film's narrative. The bride is clearly identified in a conventional dress but appears unconventional and shares similar characteristics with the other characters.

The colour codes suggest a romantic comedy; however, the enigma codes suggest that the film has other elements.

Web pages

If web pages are selected for the MS1 examination they will be presented in print format for Question 1. However, it is also important that you are familiar with web pages as moving images and that you can employ the appropriate vocabulary for analysing these media texts. Web pages are also useful examples for the representation and audience questions on this paper. Websites exist for all aspects of the media and engage a modern audience/**user** in different ways. They have a range of features that are very different to other types of media text. Their aim is to engage audiences with a short concentration span who may be 'surfing'. It is important that the content, design and layout of the site attracts the audience and encourages them to come back for more.

What are the key features of a web page?

- Navigational features – these are displayed clearly on the web page in order to help the user to move easily around the site. They are the key areas that the web designers want the audience to focus on.

- Title/banner headline – this works in the same way as headlines in magazines and newspapers do – it draws in the audience. If the headline is, for example, the name of a band, then the font style of the banner may give a clue to the music genre.

- Flash elements – these are the animations and moving elements of the site including roll overs.

- Banner advertisements – these, along with **pop-ups** are the most common form of Internet advertising and appear at the top of web pages. These will sometimes be examples of **contextual advertising** and therefore more likely to be successful. The user will click on the banner and a full version of the advert will appear.

- Multimedia features – websites will use a mixture of text, images and sound.

- External web links – an image or a key word that will take the user to another page or website.

- Interactive features – these are the elements of the website that allow the user to become involved with the site through blogs, forums, surveys, email opportunities, etc. This feature may encourage the user to return regularly to the site as their involvement develops.

Key Terms

User = This is another term for a type of audience and suggests that this audience is active and involved in the media text in some way. Some media texts, e.g. websites and computer games, encourage interactivity.

Pop-ups = These are a type of Internet advertisement where an advert literally 'pops up' on the screen when the web page is being used. Their aim is to attract web traffic or capture email addresses.

Contextual advertising = This is a form of targeted advertising where, as a result of the information the user has entered on the site, a related advert will appear.

quickfire

⑪ What opportunities do web pages offer users that print-based texts do not?

Task

Analyse a range of different websites considering the key features used to attract a user.

An example of a pop-up advert

Key Term

Media platform = This is a range of different ways of communicating, e.g. television, newspapers, Internet, etc.

Many media texts that exist in print form also have websites. These websites offer additional opportunities for new and existing users. Magazines, in particular, have exploited this **platform** to extend their audience range. Consider the features used by the magazine *Kerrang!* to attract users.

The banner advert is directly linked to the interests of the users of this site.

The navigation bar allows the user to select a range of areas including 'tickets' and 'shop'. This allows the band to promote tours and sell merchandising.

The banner headline replicates that of the print text and suggests the music genre associated with the magazine in its use of black and white and the 'shattered' font style.

www.kerrang.com,
Bauer Consumer Media Ltd

Examiner tip

Ensure that when you are analysing a media text you need to have learned and then use the relevant specialist language for that text. For example, a website has its own terminology for its key features.

quickfire

⑫ What interactive opportunities are there for a website user?

The multimedia features include podcasts, a chance to download music and an exclusive video, suggesting that the users of the site will get elements not available to the readers of the magazine.

The pop-ups and tour adverts are featured on the page with the use of the imperative 'book now' to hook the audience.

The use of a dark colour scheme has connotations of more serious music. This is reinforced by the performers featured. It is targeted at a specific audience.

The user can log on to the 'noise letter' again using a pun to link to the music genre and offering interactive opportunities to keep up to date.

The main images are of performers 'in action' suggesting that the magazine had access at the festival it is reviewing and therefore is up to date with the music scene. There is a sense of immediacy about the page.

There is iconic representation of the latest issues of the print magazine.

The layout and design is 'busy' and incorporates both text and images. The copy content suggests that the user is an informed audience who are familiar with the music scene.

Newspapers

A range of different newspapers are published in the United Kingdom. However, newspapers are no longer only available in a print form. In order to address the changing ways in which people access news and to survive in a multimedia world where audiences want information in bite-sized chunks, newspapers are now also available in non-print formats e.g. online. However, print newspapers and, in particular, their front pages still have a role to play in how we receive the news on a daily basis.

Although newspapers are dealing in facts, they are not, as some audiences may assume, '**windows on the world**'. In fact, all news is **constructed**. How the producers of the newspaper decide to present a news story will depend on the style of the newspaper, its **ideology** and the audience that will read the text. The same news is available to all the newspapers every day. How do they decide what to publish in their paper?

Choosing the news: news values

Gatekeepers decide which stories are newsworthy. News values are the criteria that will influence the decisions made by the owners, editors and journalists about which stories will appear in their newspaper. These decisions are made every day as the news is selected and constructed for the audience. An editor will only choose those stories that will interest the reader of that paper; this is the **news agenda** for the paper. Although not all news values are relevant today some of the criteria still used are:

- Threshold: the bigger the story the more likely it is to get onto the news agenda. A demonstration may only get onto the agenda if it becomes violent.

- Negativity: bad news is more exciting and interesting than good news.

- Unexpectedness: an event that is a shock or out of the ordinary, e.g. the Twin Towers attack. An event like this will push other news stories off the agenda.

- Unambiguity: events that are easy to report and are not complex will be higher up the agenda of some newspapers. Modern wars are often difficult to report and are avoided by tabloid newspapers unless they involve personalities.

- Personalisation: news stories that have a human interest angle are more likely to appear in some newspapers. Readers are interested in celebrities, and stories have more meaning if they are personal.

- Proximity: the closer to home the story is, the more interested the reader. This may mean a local event for a local paper or something pertinent to Britain in a national newspaper.

- Elite nations/people: stories about important people and powerful nations, e.g. the USA, will be higher up the agenda.

- Continuity/currency: stories that are already in the news continue to run and are updated as new aspects to the story appear, e.g. the Royal Wedding dominated the news in early 2011.

Different newspapers present stories in different ways. One of the ways in which we differentiate between newspapers in Britain is 'tabloid' and 'broadsheet'. These terms originally referred to the size of the newspaper and later, the style. This is less helpful now when *The Times* is tabloid in size and *The Guardian* introduced a new size: the Berliner. Tabloid newspapers now tend to be described as 'popular' and broadsheets as 'quality'.

If newspaper pages or website pages are set for the MS1 examination then the expectation is that you will be able to analyse them using appropriate terminology and demonstrating an understanding of the more complex issues surrounding layout and design, news selection and construction.

Key Terms

Window on the world = This is the suggestion that news programmes and documentaries offer a realistic representation of what is going on in the world.

Construction = This is how the news story is put together. The way in which it is constructed will affect how the audience responds to it. Elements of the construction may include: the caption, the choice of image and the language used to represent the aspects of the story.

Ideology = The values and messages held by the producers of a media text that may appear in the text itself. In the case of newspapers, it may be clear from the stories chosen in, for example, *The Daily Mail*, what that paper thinks about asylum seekers or the Euro.

Gatekeepers = These are the people responsible for deciding which stories will appear in the newspaper. They are usually the editor and senior journalists. They will open the gate for some stories and shut it for others.

News agenda = This is the list of news stories that may appear in a particular newspaper. Some stories of the day will never appear on the agenda of certain newspapers because they will not interest their readers. For example, whether or not Katie Price will marry again would not be on the news agenda of *The Daily Telegraph*.

Key Terms

Plug/puff = These appear in all newspapers and usually run across the top of the front page. Their aim is to show what else is in the paper and will usually contrast to the serious news on the front page to broaden the audience appeal.

Hyperbole = This is over-exaggerated language used to make the story more exciting and dramatic.

Strap lines = These are mostly found on tabloids where the headline does not give much information about the story. The strap line gives more information about the main story.

Anchorage = This is the caption or wording that accompanies an image and suggests the meaning of the image. It may also suggest the ideology of the producers of the text. It 'closes' the meaning of the image. An image without a caption is 'open' and therefore may be interpreted in different ways by the audience.

Ethnocentric = If a newspaper is ethnocentric then it tends to be concerned with issues that are close to home and will more directly interest the readers. For example, a local newspaper may only run a national or international story if a local person is involved.

⑬ How could you use this example to cover other areas of the MS1 specification?

Consider how the same story is presented in different newspapers

The Sun is a 'red top' newspaper. The masthead incorporates the icon of the poppy suggesting their patriotism.

The **plug/puff** targets a broader audience but is still 'light' in its content. A pun is used for further entertainment.

The 'exclusive' tag is an audience hook – they may buy this paper if they think they will not get this story anywhere else.

The language used in the sub-heading is emotive and the use of the term 'riot' and not 'protest' suggests the ideology of the paper and what it thinks of the event.

The headline is dramatic and not informative. It uses **hyperbole**. The large font draws attention to it immediately. The **strap line** is underlined for effect and provides an **anchorage** for the image. The use of the abbreviations 'uni', and the slang 'yobs', gives a negative representation of the students and an informal mode of address.

'Quality' newspapers are usually more formal in their style and their mode of address. The expectation of the reader of such a newspaper is that they want more information and detail about the stories. 'Quality' newspapers are generally less **ethnocentric** and will report in more detail on international and political news. Their news agendas will be different to those of a tabloid, popular paper. The front pages of quality newspapers are text-led and the images are of higher quality. They are less concerned with celebrity gossip and focus more on the key news of the day.

Consider how the style of the newspaper and the treatment of the story differs

The plug/puff broadens the appeal but suggests a more intellectual reader.

The headline is a direct quotation and is serious and enigmatic in tone.

The bullet points give more information and place the event in context.

The term 'student action' is less inflammatory than the terms used in *The Sun*. The reference to the policing problems is also more low key rather than apportioning blame.

The **copy** is much more detailed – it gives an explanation and offers a more balanced report of the event.

The image is very similar to that in *The Sun* but the readers view it differently because of the caption which anchors the image.

The right-hand column gives an opinion of the situation and allows the reader to respond to the facts.

Key Term

Copy = This is the writing in the body of the newspaper.

⑭ What news values have been considered in choosing this front page story?

CD covers

The CD covers and inserts are an important part of the way in which the performer creates their star image. It is a means by which they can market themselves to an existing and new audience. Of the many images circulating of a performer, the CD cover is one that they and their producers have control over. Most CD covers, as with other media texts, follow a set of codes and conventions and are produced in a format that is easily recognisable for the target audience. These include the following.

A central image

This may be a photograph of the performer, art work or an image related to the theme of the CD. If the image is of the performer then the mode of address may be direct in order to attract the attention of the audience. The iconography surrounding the image and the visual codes may encode clues as to the genre and style of the music. For example, *Linkin Park* use urban settings on their CD covers to suggest the seriousness and modernity of their music.

Star image

Consider how the image of the star has been **constructed** on the front cover. All the aspects of the image presented will have been carefully considered in order to transmit a set of messages to the audience. It may be that the star is introducing a new image to the audience through the visual codes that are included on the cover. These may include codes of clothing, expression and colour. There may be a **USP** associated with the CD cover that will attract the audience.

Design and layout

The design features, font styles and lettering may reflect the music genre of the performer or the theme of the CD. For example, on Katy Perry's CD cover *Teenage Dream*, the font colours and style resemble pink and white candy sticks and modelling balloons reflecting a recurring theme for this artist. The artist herself is lying on a cloud in a blue sky reflecting the dreamlike quality of the music theme. Her nudity contrasts with the seemingly girlish design elements.

Genre

One aim of the CD cover is to communicate the genre of the music to a potential audience. This may be done through a combination of images and visual codes associated with the style of music. Marilyn Manson's make up, jewellery, dark colour scheme and Gothic font style firmly places him within the Goth genre on his *Tainted Love* CD cover.

baranq/Shutterstock.com

As well as the genre conventions that are incorporated on the CD cover and suggest the style of music, CD covers as texts have a repertoire of elements that makes them recognisable to an audience and therefore fulfil audience expectations. These include the name of the band/artist, the record label, the track listings, advisory warnings, spine information, etc. The front of the CD is the aspect of the text that will first attract the attention of the audience. The back of the CD is usually less 'busy' but contains important information.

Key Term

Direct mode of address = If this is used in the text, then the person in the text is looking directly at the audience. The effect of this can differ according to the text and the expression used. The direct mode of address may make the audience feel involved and 'invited into' the text, or it may make them feel challenged and uncomfortable. The audience response will also change according to whether they are the intended audience for the text.

Examiner tip

Consider how one text could be used to answer more than one question of the examination paper. CD covers may not be the stimulus material for Q1, but these examples can be used in a response to a representation or audience question.

The image of the performer on a CD cover or any promotional material is important. The artist Snoop Dogg promotes a particular image on his CD covers. His mode of address on, for example, the CD cover *Rhythm & Gangsta* is serious and challenging as a smile would not reflect the star's persona. If you study this CD cover you will see that the iconography used within the image is conventional of the genre – the hoodie, the bling and the use of archaic style writing. There is also the inclusion of the stereotypical woman as an accessory to the star

In this text the colours, use of images and visual codes suggest a different music genre. The handwriting style personalises the text. The hand-drawn images and water-colour effect suggest a dream-like, romantic quality and the use of pastel colours and blurred images emphasises this. The title of the CD is enigmatic and intriguing for the audience. The fact that the artist is not featured adds to this.

John McKeown, 'Things worth fighting for', Beat Route Records

Computer games covers

The aim of computer games covers, like DVD covers and film posters, is to promote the game and to give an audience a taste of what they will experience when they purchase the game. Games covers, like the other examples of texts analysed, have a set of codes and conventions which include:

- A central image that attracts the attention of the **user**. This may be similar to that used on other publicity material. If the game is part of a series then the user may recognise the characters and/or the style of artwork used.

- Characters – these may be recognisable to the users of the game. For example, Ezio Auditore from the *Assassin's Creed* series who has a distinctive costume and appearance related to the game's theme, genre and historical time period.

- Narrative – the cover will give narrative **teasers** and **enigmas** to persuade the audience that they want to play the game. These may be the plot situations included in the **thumbnails** that usually appear on the back of the games cover. There will also be a **story synopsis** on the back cover that will be delivered in dramatic and often hyperbolic language.

- Tag line/slogan – as on a film poster, this will sum up the game. The tag line for *Fifa 12* is 'Love football. Play football' suggesting user involvement.

- Expert comments – these may include quotes from reviews included in games magazines, newspapers, etc.

- **Subject-specific lexis** – an understanding of the language used involves 'real' gamers and excludes others. For example, 'experience open world gameplay'.

- Setting and iconography – the game cover will suggest where the game is set and will have appropriate iconography. *Assassin's Creed* is set in Italian locations and includes iconic graphic representations of Venice and Florence from, apparently, 1476. The artwork for this game, as with other games, is of a high standard.

- Technical codes – the covers will include a range of camera shots and angles to simulate a filmic experience for the user. The screenshots will also give an idea of the interactivity of the game.

- Language and mode of address – this may directly address the user and include lexis related to gameplay. It will also give the user promises of pleasure involved with playing the game 'use new assassin's skills and allies to defeat your enemies' (*Assassin's Creed 2*). This reinforces the interactive opportunities of the game.

- Industry information – this will include the certification, the name and logo of the producer, the format and any warnings regarding use of the game.

Key Terms

User = The term 'user' suggests involvement and interactivity. The audience of a game 'uses' the text – they make choices and decisions that affect their progress and are therefore active rather than passive.

Teasers/enigmas = These are clues to what happens in the game. Some of the information is withheld from the user so that they will want to purchase the game to find the answers.

Thumbnails = These are the small drawings that represent the plot situations from the game. They usually appear on the back of the game cover.

Story synopsis = This is the summing up of the storyline to give the user an idea of what happens in the game.

Subject-specific lexis = This is the language used in a media text that relates specifically to that text. Non-users of the text will not understand the language and therefore will be distanced from the text. Those who understand will feel involved in the world of the text.

⑮ What techniques are used by the creators of games covers to attract users?

Screenshots from L.A. Noire,
Rockstar Games

Key Terms

Film noir = This was a style, rather than genre of films from the 1940s and 50s that had common cinematic features including low-key lighting. They were crime dramas involving recognisable character types and settings.

Chiaroscuro lighting = Low-key lighting used to create areas of light and darkness, particularly in black and white films. The effect is to suggest unease and tension within the scene.

Femme fatale = This was the female character in a film noir. Her main characteristics were that she was beautiful, seductive, amoral and able to manipulate the male protagonist to do her will. She was usually destroyed at the end of the film.

The computer games industry is continuing to grow, and audiences are demanding more from the games produced. This demand was met in 2011 when Rockstar Games launched *L.A. Noire* for Playstation 3 and Xbox 360. *L.A. Noire* is a crime video game and is set in Los Angeles in 1947. The iconography and narrative of the game takes its inspiration from the **film noir** genre of the 1940s and 50s. This is also evident in the highly acclaimed art work and style of the game. In the game the player is a detective in control of the LA Police Department and has to solve a range of cases.

- The front and back of the cover are in black and white and colour – the gameplay also has this option (www.youtube.com/watch?v=0sk9YjbbyJw).

- The thumbnails suggest plot situations synonymous with the genre of film noir. They are presented as still 'crime scene' photographs. The anchorage accompanying them suggests the American crime film 'homicide', 'corpses', 'detective'.

- The narrative is presented through the tag line 'There are cases that make you... and others that break you'. The use of the personal pronoun suggests the role of the user as the detective.

- The iconography suggests the genre and the period: the code of clothing, guns and the urban setting.

- The setting echoes that of film noir – fog and dark streets.

- The lighting is **chiaroscuro**, again reflecting the genre.

- The characters include the detective who is placed centrally on the cover. The woman is represented as the **'femme fatale'** but is also seen as the victim. The enigmatic character on the back cover is faceless and is seen replacing his gun thus creating an enigma.

- The producers of the game are given a high profile on the front cover as they will be recognisable as creators of other games including *Grand Theft Auto*.

- The industry information includes the games developers Team Bondi, the certification and other related information.

Grade boost

Learn and use the relevant technical terminology when analysing a media text.

Key Terms

Zoo format = This is a style of radio programme where there is a main presenter but also others who contribute. The mode of address is informal and there are jokes and chat between the participants. A radio programme that uses this format is Radio Two's *Big Show* with Steve Wright.

Magazine programme = This is a genre of radio programme that, like a magazine, includes a range of features, for example music, chat, news, gossip and interviews.

Profile = With regard to radio stations, this means how they would be defined. This may include their target audience, their aims and their ethos. For example, the profile for Radio 1 is to

'entertain and engage a broad range of young listeners with a distinctive mix of contemporary music and speech. Its target audience is 15–29 year olds and it should also provide some programming for younger teenagers.

It should offer a range of new music, support emerging artists – especially those from the UK – and provide a platform for live music. News, documentaries and advice campaigns should cover areas of relevance to young adults.'

www.bbc.co.uk/aboutthebbc/
statements2010/radio/radio1.shtml

Grade boost

Make sure that you have listened to radio programmes across a range of stations and not just the ones you usually tune in to. Radio stations can be useful texts to use when discussing audience targeting.

Radio extracts

In the MS1 examination paper you may be given a radio extract as stimulus material. You may also want to use a radio extract as an example to illustrate points made about representation or audience.

The role and purpose of radio has changed significantly over recent years. It has been affected by advances in digital technology including the ability of the audience to listen online, to download podcasts to their mobile phones and to see radio programmes as they are recorded through studio webcams. Digital Audio Broadcasting (DAB) provides ease of use and better sound quality. The medium of radio consists of:

- **The blind medium** – it only involves the sense of hearing with no visual images. In this sense it allows the audience to use their imagination.

- **The companion medium** – the radio format provides a strong sense of personal communication for the audience. It also offers interactive opportunities – audiences can text and email programmes and get a 'mention' or a 'shout out' on the radio programme.

- **The intimate medium** – radio is very personal. It encourages intimacy by the use of the direct mode of address.

- **The undemanding medium** – it allows the audience to do other things while listening.

All radio programmes focus on the human voice, whether speaking or singing. They also have a clear narrative structure even when the programme appears unscripted and improvised. Many programmes are presenter led and often audiences will 'tune in' because they like the style of a particular presenter, which may have been established over a period of time. Terry Wogan, until his recent retirement from the Radio Two breakfast slot, commanded very high listening figures mainly due to his particular style of presentation. The **zoo format** is a particular style of a radio **magazine programme** and tends to actively involve audiences and has a broad reach due to the range of features included.

The genre of radio programmes can be divided into speech-based and music-based. Most radio stations offer a schedule that includes a range of genres, although the **profile** of some radio stations, for example Radio One and *Kerrang* Radio, is generally music-based. The profile of the radio station will dictate the types of programme aired and will define the target audience who, as in the case of television, will have expectations of what the radio station will provide. The audience for radio stations is often defined by the age of the listener. Radio 1 tends to cater for a younger audience who are less interested in speech-based radio, whereas Radio Four focuses on speech-based programmes and targets an older demographic. The codes and conventions of speech-based programmes include:

- Phone-ins. These are effective, cheap ways of involving the listener. Jeremy Vine's lunchtime radio programme on Radio Two revolves around music, discussion and listeners phoning in to give their opinions about current issues and events in the news.

- Discussions – a group of people sitting around discussing a range of topics. This genre of programme is often a key part of Radio Four's schedule.

- Outside broadcasts – mobile studios may visit different locations and broadcast from there. For example, this summer, Radio One had a live broadcast from Glastonbury where recognisable radio personalities like Jo Whiley gave first-hand experience of the festival for those listening at home.

- Drama – Radio Four has a regular feature of *The Afternoon Play*. Other dramas include the long-running radio soap *The Archers*.

- Programmes are generally **stripped** across the schedules to appeal to different audiences at different times of the day.

- The programmes reflect the profile of the station. They are speech-based and address a highbrow audience. However, Radio 4 does also air comedy programmes usually stripped across the schedules at 6.30 pm.

On the majority of radio stations music is the main focus. Most stations air their music programmes at specific times during the day related to what listeners will be doing. For example, breakfast shows and **drive time programmes**. The features of music-led programmes include:

- **Presenter-led programmes** – this is the most popular format on stations like Radio 1 and 2. Here the personality of the presenter is as important as the music and they will bring with them their fan base and the programme will have a particular **house style**. This is the case with the breakfast shows on Radio 1 and 2 hosted by Chris Moyles and Chris Evans respectively. Chris Moyles is known for his 'laddish' approach and often controversial humour. These programmes will have a clear format and listeners will know what to expect at specific times during the programme.

Key Terms

Stripping = This is a scheduling technique used in radio and television whereby the same programme or genre of programme is scheduled at the same time every day.

Drive time programmes = These are the programmes that are scheduled between 5 and 7 pm and are designed for listeners who are driving home.

House style = For a radio programme this means the style of the programme which may include: jingles, presenter mode of address, content and music genres played.

Still taken from YouTube – The Chris Moyles Show 50hr Broadcast, *BBC Radio 1*

16 Consider how *The Chris Moyles Show* on Radio 1 could be used as an example of representation of gender in the media today, if used as an example for a representation question.

- **Zoo format**. Often the main presenter will have a support team who will engage in informal chat and gossip and give their opinions on a range of events and issues of relevance to the target audience.

- **Live concerts** – these can be of popular performers or of orchestras (usually aired on Radio 3).

- **Session programmes** – here bands and artists are invited into the studio and part of a regular programme would be devoted to the performer playing live. The presenter will also usually interview the performer.

- **Music documentaries** – here programmes will be devoted to an analysis of the output and life of a particular musician; for example, after the death of Amy Winehouse there were several radio documentaries made celebrating her brand of music.

- **Personal choice programmes** – for example *Desert Island Discs* on Radio 4, where celebrities choose their favourite music.

Film trailers

The stimulus material for MS1 Question 1 may be film trailers or extracts from films, for example an opening sequence. Film trailers are rich texts containing many features for analysis. They are an important way in which the film industry markets their product. Their purpose is to raise audience expectations so that they will want to go and see the film. The main codes and conventions are:

- The name of the film. This will usually feature prominently in the trailer. If the film is new then the name may give a clue to the film's genre, for example. If it is a sequel then the audience will already be aware of the genre, for example, *Scream 2.*

- The use of graphics to reinforce the name of the film and its stars. The font style may help to establish the film's genre. Here the name of the film is bold and is surrounded by a dark, stormy sky giving connotations of action and power associated with the word.

Still taken from Thor *trailer, director Kenneth Branagh, Marvel Studios (2011)*

- The main characters. These are often introduced using technical codes, for example close-ups, to establish them in the minds of the audience. A **tag line**. This may give a clue to the genre and the narrative.

- Audio codes. These may include a theme tune or sound track which may be recognisable to an audience, for example the same theme tune was used in all of the *Raiders of The Lost Ark* films. There may also be sound effects placing the film in a particular genre, for example gun shots and explosions in an action film. Atmospheric music may be used to create a mood and suggest the film's genre.

- The use of the voice-over. The purpose of this is to establish continuity between the scenes chosen for the trailer, to establish the narrative and to give **promises of pleasure** to the audience.

- **Genre-specific lexis**. This helps to tell the audience what to expect from the film.

Key Terms

Tag line = This is the catchy phrase or slogan that sums up the film and is generally used on all marketing material. For example, the tag line for the thriller *Dream House* is 'the truth can't stay inside forever'.

Promises of pleasure = This is what the trailer tells the audience they will get out of the film. They may laugh, or cry, or be more terrified than ever before!

Genre-specific lexis = This is where the trailer includes words and phrases the audience would associate with that particular genre.

Codes and conventions

- Highlighting the stars that are appearing in the film. This feature is important as some stars tend to appear in specific genres and often the star will be a key selling point of the film.

- Editing. The trailer will be constructed and the best extracts from the film will be selected to attract the audience. The chosen extracts will also establish the narrative strands in the film and may include some of the plot situations. These may be recognisable to an audience who are familiar with the genre. These stills from the trailer for *Dream House* demonstrate that the film is from the thriller/horror genre. The lighting is low key, in three of the shots the characters are only lit by lamps and are surrounded by darkness. The codes of clothing and expression represent the family as vulnerable; this is further enhanced by the mother wearing white in two shots. The iconography of the knife and the close-up shot of the scream are conventions of this genre of film. The use of the distorted reflection is also a conventional technical code and is enigmatic for the audience.

Stills taken from Dream House, *director Jim Sheridan, Universal Studios (2011)*

- Enigma codes. Trailers withhold information from the audience to encourage them to want to watch the film to find the answers. Sometimes **rhetorical questions** will be asked by the voice-over or by words appearing on the screen. For example, 'What if the mystery you were trying to solve was your own?' appears on the trailer for *Dream House*. This, combined with the narrative clues, increases the enigma effect for the audience.

- Additional information. This may include the release date and certification, for example.

Key Term

Rhetorical questions = These are questions to which an answer is not expected. The use of them in media texts like trailers serves to introduce enigmas in the minds of an audience. They will only find out the answers by watching the whole film and as such they are a marketing tool.

quickfire

(17) How are trailers constructed to attract audiences to the film? Back up your points with specific examples.

Grade boost

When analysing a trailer, remember that they are rich texts that contain a range of different features. Ensure that you analyse the text using appropriate terminology and avoid 'telling the story'.

Television extracts

The stimulus material for the MS1 examination may be an extract from a television programme. Remember you will be given bullet points to guide you with the focus of your answer. The extracts can be from any genre and may be opening sequences, trailers for programmes or extracts from within the programme itself. You will have watched examples in class and you need to transfer your analytical skills to the examples given in the examination.

Codes and conventions of television programmes

Still taken from YouTube – Credit Sequence, Waking the Dead *BBC (2000–2011)*

- The credit sequence – if you are shown an extract that includes the credit sequence, consider what is communicated through this sequence about the programme. For example, in the credit sequence for *Waking The Dead*, a BBC forensic crime drama, the iconography includes fingerprints, hairs and microscopes thus placing the programme clearly in its genre. The lighting is also low key, suggesting that the subject matter is 'dark' and hidden. The programme's title and the characters' names are indistinct and move in and out of focus as if a microscope is moving over the letters, creating an enigma and reinforcing the genre.

- The narrative – consider how it is established in the extract. Are there obvious narrative strands that are introduced? Does a key event happen in the extract? How is the narrative conveyed? (Look back at the section on narrative.) For example, if the editing is fast paced then this would suggest an action genre. In what way do the technical codes communicate the narrative? For example, the opening sequence of a television drama like *Spooks* starts with a short montage of shots reminding the audience of what happened in the last episode. The audience can then anticipate what is to come.

- Iconography – this is a clue to the genre of the programme. The clothing, setting, objects and backgrounds may be relevant to the question. In a forensic crime drama, the audience may expect to see characters dressed in white coats, scene of crime tape, gritty, urban settings and objects related to the extraction of evidence, for example tweezers.

- Characters – certain television genres have a set of characters that an audience expects to see. These may be central **protagonists** and **stock**, support **characters**. The audience can anticipate the behaviour of these characters and can predict how they will react in certain narratives. You may be asked to comment on the characters if a television extract is the stimulus for MS1, Question 1. Ensure that you discuss their codes of clothing, gesture and expression as well as their role within the narrative and their relationship with other characters.

Still from Waking the Dead, *Series 6, series producer Colin Wratten, director Marc Joubst, BBC (2008)*

- Technical codes. Different television programmes will employ a range of different technical codes. Documentary programmes may use a direct mode of address to more forcefully convey the programme's message and to engage directly with the audience. Soap operas and other dramas dealing with relationships may employ close-ups to position the audience with regard to the characters.

Still from Ross Kemp on Gangs: San Salvador, *Series 2, executive producer Clive Tulloh, Tiger Aspect Productions (2006)*

- Audio codes. Just as different genres of television programme employ certain technical codes, the audio codes also convey messages to the audience. Soap operas have distinctive opening theme tunes that have changed little over many years as audiences are familiar with them and they signal the start of the programme. The ending drum beat of *EastEnders* often synchronises with a narrative cliffhanger. Situation comedies use **canned laughter** to signal to audiences what they should find amusing in the programme. The dialogue included in the programme will also give clues to the narrative and the genre.

Key Terms

Protagonist = The key character in a film or television programme. The protagonist will be central to the narrative and influence its development through their actions and relationships with other characters.

Stock characters = Easily recognisable characters, often stereotypes who support the main characters.

Canned laughter = This is pre-recorded laughter that is added to a television or radio programme post-production. It serves to prompt the audience and encourage them to laugh at the funny bits of the programme.

Examiner tip

Many students neglect audio in their analysis. Always remember to listen to the audio and analyse why it has been included and its effect upon an audience.

 quicKfire

⑱ Study the still from *Waking the Dead*. Analyse the characters and the iconography.

Music videos

The stimulus material for MS1 may be a music video. The music video is an important promotional tool used by the music industry to market performers and their music. It also helps to create the 'star image' for a new performer and adapts or develops the image of a more established music artist. The music video is also used to interpret and anchor the meaning of a song and to entertain an audience through a range of strategies. The iconography employed in the music video may also give an indication of the style of the performer and the genre of the music. Music videos can differ in style and can be:

- Performance

- Narrative

- Thematic, related to the song lyrics

- A combination of more than one of the above.

Performance music videos

Early music videos developed from clips of bands and artists in performance. Today, many music videos include the performance of the artist as part of the video. This can be for different reasons: for a serious band that create and play their own music, the performance element of it will demonstrate their musical skill: for an artist like Rihanna, her 'performance' skills may be used to develop her **star persona** and to attract a wide audience of both genders. The codes and conventions of performance videos include:

- Clips from live stage performances with shots of the artists performing and shots of the audience. This gives the audience at home a sense of atmosphere and involvement.

- Shots of the artists in 'real-life' situations, for example warming up, messing about. This gives the audience access to a more personal view of the performers, even if it is still constructed for this purpose.

- Lots of close-ups of the performer who may have a direct mode of address in order to engage the audience. Music videos of this style can also be referred to as 'a spectacle' with direct interaction with the audience.

- The close-ups may also be of iconography suggesting the music genre or the theme of the song. Sometimes an artist has a particular recognisable **motif** that is echoed throughout videos.

- To add entertainment value, the artists may perform in unusual places and will be lip-synched, for example on roof tops, in fields, etc.

Key Terms

Star persona = This term is used to refer to those music stars that have an identity beyond their ability to make music. That persona may be demonstrated through character and personality and be evident in other media texts, for example magazine interviews, advertising campaigns, etc. Some stars are adept at changing their star persona to keep fans interested; this is true of Madonna and Lady Gaga. The producer of the star may be instrumental in creating their persona.

Motif = This is a current thematic element used by an artist and recognised by fans of that artist. It is usually established by the iconography surrounding the artist including props, costumes and settings. A good example is Katy Perry's *Candy-Coated Tour*. Her singles from this time and her music videos repeated the motifs of sweets, candy sticks, hundreds and thousands, pink hair, etc., to suggest a controversial girlish sexuality.

quickfire

⑲ What elements of performance music video are evident in the examples illustrated?

Still from Greatest Day, *Take That;*
Polydor (2008)

Still from You and I, *Lady Gaga;*
Streamline/Interscope records (2011)

Still from The Catalyst *Linkin Park;*
Warner Bros (2010)

Music videos: the narrative music video

Another genre of music video is the narrative music video. Here the performer's aim is to take the audience through the story of their music in some of the following ways:

- Filming and **editing** that tells the story featured or suggested in the lyrics. This narrative may surprise the audience by giving a different interpretation from the one most obviously suggested by the song lyrics.

- The construction of a narrative that may involve the performer playing themselves or a character they have created. Alternatively, the artist may not appear and the characters in the story may all be actors.

- The creation of a narrative that is like a mini film. The production values may be high depending on the success of the band/performer. It may have a clear linear structure or may be a series of seemingly unrelated narrative events.

- A narrative that may contain enigmas to maintain the attention of the audience.

- Stereotypical representations of characters that communicate the story effectively to the audience.

- Elements of **intertextuality**. Taylor Swift's music video for her song *You Belong to Me* uses the Cinderella story and establishes clear stereotypes of American high school teenagers and a 'femme fatale'.

Key Terms

Editing = The editing techniques of music videos are usually visually stylish and at times, artistic. The editing is fast paced allowing only a short time to build up meaning. The cutting and editing can often link to the rhythm of the music. Music videos also often break the rules of continuity editing in an attempt to grab the attention of the audience and to be innovative.

Intertextuality = Using one text within another. For example, the use of a fairytale within a music video. Gwen Stefani uses the narrative features of *Rapunzel* in her music video *The Sweet Escape*.

Stills from You Belong To Me, *Taylor Swift; Big Machine Records (2009)*

- Some music videos will use a combination of narrative edited together with the shots of the artist performing to enhance the audience experience and to remind them of the various facets of the performer. In Katy Perry's music video *Hot and Cold* there is a clear linear narrative interspersed with clips of Perry performing as various personas within the story. Her representation in this music video is one of power and dominance over the male protagonist. The iconography changes at various stages of the storyline emphasising her control and the bridegroom's vulnerability. This video also takes on the stereotypical narrative structure of the dream.

Grade boost

If music videos are set as the stimulus material for the MS1 examination, it is important that you analyse the codes and conventions of the music video focussing upon the bullet points given. These may direct you to discuss narrative codes, genre and technical codes. Avoid just telling the story.

Stills from Hot and Cold, *Katy Perry; Capitol Music (2008)*

Key Terms

A range of texts = These may include:
Advertisements
DVD covers
CD covers
Newspaper front pages
Magazines (including comics)
Radio sequences
Film extracts
Television sequences
Music videos
Websites (for the purposes of the examination, these will be reproduced in print format)
Computer game extracts

Textual analysis = The expectation is that you will be able to analyse the text chosen for the stimulus material in detail using the bullet points to guide you.

Summary and approaches to MS1 Question 1

Key points to remember

- Question 1 is a '**textual analysis**' question. You will be given some unseen stimulus material to analyse.

- The stimulus material used in the examination will be selected from a variety of different media texts.

- You will be given bullet points to guide you in your response. Make sure that you respond to all the bullet points in your answer.

- If the stimulus material is moving image, you will see the extract once and you must not make notes. You will then see the extract again during which you may make notes, you will then be given 10 minutes for further note-taking before you see the extract for a final time.

Approaches to the question

- You will be given reading time at the beginning of the examination. Make sure that you read all of the questions but, at this stage, particularly questions 1, 2a and b as these will all refer to the stimulus material.

- Make sure that you make useful notes that will help you to answer the questions. Grids and tables are useful ways in which you can record your ideas and analytical points.

- Make sure that you do not only describe what you see. Remember to comment on the purpose and effect of techniques used in the texts. For example, if you are analysing a film sequence and you want to comment on the use of a close-up shot, explain why the shot was used at that particular point in the film and what the effect on the audience might be.

- Use relevant media and analytical terminology. Make sure that you know the correct vocabulary to allow you to analyse different media texts.

- Make sure that you remember your essay-writing skills. Your response should be logical and coherent. It must also be written in sentences and paragraphed correctly. It is important that your response has a structure and includes an introduction and a conclusion.

wavebreakmedia ltd/Shutterstock.com

Representation

What do we mean by representation?

In the context of Media Studies, this means the way in which aspects of society, including gender, age, ethnicity and national/local identity, are presented to an audience by specific media texts. It is also important to consider how events and issues are presented in the media and what effect that may have upon the response of the audience. The way in which these areas are represented will change according to the **context**. The following questions are important to bear in mind when considering the concept of **representation**.

Key questions

- What kind of world is represented by the media text? Is what it presents as reality a construction?

- How are stereotypes used in the text? What is their purpose?

- Who is in control of the text? Are there any ideas and values apparent in the representations, e.g. all Geordies are chavs?

- Who is the target audience of the text? Will different audiences respond to the representations in different ways? Will people in Newcastle respond differently to the above representation from those in London?

- What messages are contained within the text?

Encoding and decoding

The media are very powerful and the way in which they represent key areas of society, issues and events directly links to the ways in which audiences interpret, understand and respond. Repetition by a media text of a particular representation over time makes that representation appear to be 'normal'. For example, front covers of women's magazines continually bombard audiences with unrealistic images of perfect women. The producers of a media text **encode** ideas and messages through the representations contained within the text. The audience then **decode** the messages and may respond to them in a range of different ways. The way in which women are represented in magazines may be accepted by some audiences who will 'buy into' the message regarding body size. Other readers may challenge or ignore that message and will decode the text differently extracting from it what matters most to them.

All media texts, both factual and fictional, are constructed. They offer versions of reality that have gone through a process of mediation. The constructions contain messages and will be interpreted differently by different audiences. The ideology of the creators will often be encoded into the constructed representations. The Toolkit you need to be able to effectively discuss representation as a concept is as follows.

Key Terms

Context = Where the representation appears, e.g. the representation of young people may be different in a news bulletin compared to a situation comedy.

Representation = The ways in which the media present the world and aspects of it, e.g. people, issues, events, etc.

Encoding = The ideas and messages that are contained within the media text. These may reflect the ideas of the producers of the text.

Decoding = The different ways in which the audience interprets these messages.

20 **What effect can the representations contained within media texts have upon audiences?**

Grade boost

Remember to demonstrate your understanding that the representations in media texts do not reflect reality.

Key Terms

Fly on the wall documentary = This term describes a documentary programme filmed using hidden cameras. The suggestion is that the subjects of the film will behave more naturally and as a result reality will be captured.

Selection = This is what is chosen by the creators of the text to be included in the text. This selection may reflect the ideology of the text and decisions have been made about what to include and what to leave out.

Editorial = This is the part of the newspaper written, supposedly, by the editor who comments on the day's stories. It offers an opportunity for the paper to express its views and to demonstrate its ideology.

Grade boost

You will be asked to demonstrate your understanding of the concept of representation in either Questions 2c or 3 of the MS1 exam paper. It is important that you are able to present an overview and to use appropriate vocabulary.

Construction

The aspects that make up any media text will have been constructed to achieve an effect. This finished construction, particularly in factual texts, gives an illusion of reality that becomes accepted by an audience as the truth. The **documentary, fly on the wall** section of a programme like *Strictly Come Dancing* constructs a narrative that positions the audience through the editing of film footage. The hours of film have been edited down to present a particular view of a character or situation in order to manipulate the emotions of the audience. For the programme *Educating Essex*, the hidden cameras were placed in the school for several weeks and the final episodes of the programme were constructed from that footage. Characters were focussed upon and narratives were created but we were not seeing real life in that school, we were seeing a selected representation.

Mediation

This relates to construction and **selection** and is the process that a text may go through before it is consumed by an audience. In the riots of August 2011, the news of the events came from a range of different sources and then appeared on the front page of newspapers. With a story like this the audience at home have to rely on how the event is represented and mediated as they cannot witness it first-hand. What are these mediation processes?

- Aspects of the event are captured by a camera and this immediately gives a focus through what is included and what is left out.

- One of the main front page images used was of a track-suited, hooded youth in front of a burning car, this was then anchored by a caption suggesting how the audience should view this image.

- A headline gave a further interpretation, in this case through the use of emotive and hyperbolic language including lexis like 'yobs', 'feral' and 'mob rule'.

- Within the newspaper the **editorial** may offer further opinion offering a representation of the event.

- The way in which the event was mediated through the images, text and representations of young people affects the way in which an audience may respond.

Picsfive/Shutterstock.com

Using examples of representation for MS1

For the MS1 paper 'representation' may be the focus of either Question 2c or Question 3. The areas of representation you may be asked about in the examination are:

- Gender
- Ethnicity
- Age
- Issues
- Events
- Regional and national identities.

The expectation is that in your response you will demonstrate an overview of the concept and demonstrate your understanding of representation by exploring three contrasting examples from a range of different media forms. It is important that you demonstrate an understanding of representation in terms of **context** and purpose. The representation in a media text may have a different purpose. This may change according to the type of text it is, i.e. the context. It will also be interpreted differently by audiences. For example, the representation of young people in *The Inbetweeners* is different from that of *Kidulthood* as the purpose of one is comedy and of the second is to present reality. In *The Inbetweeners*, **stereotypes** are used in order to transmit messages about characters rapidly in order that the audience will recognise the stereotypical character traits. It is from these stereotypes that the comedy evolves and the audience have expectations of how the characters will behave. They accept that they are not realistic representations but are created for a purpose.

It is important in order to access the higher grades, that the examples you use in the examination are fully developed to show your understanding of representation. It is also important that you discuss how the representation is created and constructed in your chosen examples. In a moving image text the creation of the representation involves:

- Camera shots and angles
- Editing
- Audio codes.

In print images the representation in created through:

- The layout and design
- Language and mode of address
- Camera shots and angles.

Elements of selection, construction and mediation, as discussed earlier in this section, also serve to produce the representation.

Key Terms

Context = This means where the representation appears and therefore, how the meaning is changed as a result.

Stereotypes = A stereotype is a construction whereby character traits are over-exaggerated to make them easily recognisable. Stereotypes can be positive or negative and are quick ways for the producers of media texts to transmit messages to audiences.

Grade boost

When you are answering an examination question ensure that you are writing in a coherent, structured way. Give an overview at the beginning showing your understanding of the concept of representation and of any key words contained within the question. Develop your analysis through your examples and conclude the response by summing up your main points.

Representations of age in the media today

Key Terms

Dominant ideology = This is the point of view of the creators of the media text. This may be implicit or explicit as is evident in texts like tabloid newspapers.

Opinion leaders = These are those in positions of power who aim to persuade an audience of their point of view (ideology). Within the media these may be newspaper editors, programme producers or film directors.

Young People

The way in which young people are represented in the media today is often controversial and a topic of debate, but was never more so than during the riots of August 2011. The main way in which the event was presented to the audience was through the news media and as such was mediated through the **dominant ideology** of the particular paper. The newspapers became **opinion leaders** offering a constructed view of young people and also of the events as they unfolded. As most of the audience could not have first-hand experience of the riots, they relied upon the news and newspapers as their sources of information. Language is a very powerful communicator of ideology as is apparent in these front pages:

Copyright Express Newspapers

Examiner tip

Although in this case we have considered how the coverage of the riots represented young people, this example can equally be used to explore the representation of an event in the media. This is true of many of the examples you will study. Be ready to use your examples for more than one area of the examination paper.

Task

Now consider another example of how young people are represented in the media. Make sure that it is from a different media form.

What points could you make in your response?

- Make general points in your introduction about what representation means and how representations are constructed by the media texts to elicit a response from an audience.

- Demonstrate your understanding of how the ideology of the text may affect the representation of certain groups, issues or events.

- Comment on the use of hyperbole in the headlines and the specific emotive vocabulary used in the sub-headings.

- The main image used has been specifically chosen and appeared in both of the newspapers and others on the same day. Analyse the visual codes used including the clothing in the main image and the background. Comment on how this image became iconic as a representation of young people during that event. How will audiences decode these images?

- Comment on how the images, headlines, captions and copy are all constructed to create a negative representation of young people.

- Consider the purpose and effect of the features of these front covers.

Positive representations of young people in the media are less frequent. However, it could be the case that we notice positive representations less because they are not usually as dramatic, entertaining or interesting. They also tend to appear only in certain texts. Television programmes like, for example, *Britain's Got Talent* and *The X Factor* have recently showcased young talent and offered positive representations of young people. In sport too, people like Ellie Simmonds are represented positively for their achievements and are heralded as role models for young people. Consider this alternative representation of youth in a different form.

Picture: PA

PLENTY TO SMILE ABOUT: Simmonds became Britain's youngest-ever Paralympic champion in 2008

Ellie loving life on golden pond

going to be quite hard, splitting the time between studying and training. It can be a bit daunting at times but I wouldn't swap my position for the world."

Life has changed immeasurably for Simmonds, who said: "I've had so many different experiences, such good things: getting an MBE and the BBC Young Sports Personality of the Year Award. It's all good."

Simmonds was the youngest-ever recipient of an MBE, aged 14, in the Queen's 2009 New Year's Honours and her success and positive personality have made her a perfect role model.

Now part of the scheme by sponsors Sainsbury's aimed at getting one million children to take part in a Paralympic sport, Simmonds added: "It's really important for kids to get involved in a variety of sports.

"Maybe not just competitively but to keep fit, have a healthy lifestyle. And when they're doing a particular sport, they might find where their talent lies.

"I'm proud of what I've achieved. Hopefully, people will see what I'm doing and follow in my footsteps and see that there are sports put there for them."

❑ *ELLIE SIMMONDS was at the Lee Valley Athletics Stadium for the launch of Sainsbury's 1 Million Kids Paralympics Campaign which will encourage children to give Paralympic sports a go. For more information and to take part, log on to: www. sainsburys.co.uk/1millionkids*

500 DAYS TO GO

Singer Ronan is bookies' favourite

By Giles Sheldrick

YOUNG singing sensation Ronan Parke has emerged as the bookmakers' favourite to win the grand final of Britain's Got Talent on Saturday.

Ronan, 12, held his nerve to flawlessly cover Bob Dylan's Make You Feel My Love, melting the judges' hearts and winning millions of public votes in Monday's live semi-final.

But despite earning a legion of fans – and many female admirers – the Norfolk schoolboy yesterday admitted he has only room for two women in his life, Lady Gaga and Beyonce, and certainly no time for a girlfriend.

Ronan said he dreamed of performing a duet with the chart superstars. He said: "If I could perform with anyone it would be those two – they're amazing."

He said: "I'm only 12 and thanks to Britain's Got Talent I have been recognised and asked for pictures and autographs. But I don't have a girlfriend and I'm quite happy singing."

Even acid-tongued Simon Cowell said Ronan "totally and utterly nailed" the song after Monday's performance.

Fellow judge David Hasselhoff, tipped Parke to win the competition on Saturday night.

He said: "You sang your heart out and we all felt it – you're going to be really hard to beat."

Amanda Holden said: "It was effortless. You have the most gorgeous voice and your parents must be bursting with pride – as I think the whole nation will be after that performance."

Last night a modest Ronan said "anyone could win the competition" but allowed himself to dream.

He added: "I would of course love to win. To perform for the Queen would be amazing.

"If I won the £100,000 I'd take my family away on holiday to Italy."

Ronan wants to sing for the Queen

Copyright Express Newspapers

What points could you make in your response?

- Introduce these images as alternative examples of the representation of youth in the media today and examine the context in which they appear and the audience who may consume them.

- The headline of the news stories places the image and the story in a context and positions the audience.

- Here the code of expression in the images is positive, showing smiling young people.

- The mode of address is celebratory supported by positive vocabulary. Give specific examples to back up the points you make. For example, Ellie is described as 'the youngest ever recipient of an MBE' and a 'perfect role model'. The *Daily Express* describes Ronan Parke as a 'singing sensation'.

Photographer
Trevor Leighton
©Woman &
Home/ IPC+
Syndication

quickfire

㉑ How is the dominant ideology of a media text reflected through the representations included within the text?

Examiner tip

Ageism in the media is also an issue. In your study of representations of age you need to bear that in mind and consider how you could use examples that may cover both areas of the specification. *The Dove Campaign for Real Beauty* is an example of how their representation of older women in beauty adverts was inspired by concerns about ageism in the media.

Task

Now find a third example from another media form, for example television, that offers a different representation of older people.

Older people

The representation of older ages in the media today is as equally a controversial area as that of young people. Representations of older people are often constructed in a very stereotypical way focussing on character traits including deafness, grumpiness and an inability to function effectively in society. However, it is important that your discussion of age in the examination does not, itself, become stereotypical but that you demonstrate a more sophisticated knowledge supported by a range of examples. Ageing itself is not always seen positively in the media – the emphasis in many areas of the media is upon avoiding it. In texts like glamour magazines, even when an image on an older person appears on the front cover, the cover lines usually focus upon how they have managed to look younger and how the audience can achieve that. *Woman and Home* is a useful text as it frequently features older women and their 'secrets' for looking younger. This issue has been branded the 'Age-less' issue and much of the content focuses around how to stay young. Consider how the visual codes and layout and design communicate the ideology of the magazine. How realistic a representation of an older person is Joanna Lumley? How might different audiences respond to this text?

In this text, the film *Gran Torino*, Clint Eastwood, through his character in this film, offers a more challenging representation of older people and their ideas and values. A further useful text is the DVD cover for this film. Consider how the film and the DVD cover use images, visual codes, narrative devices and iconography to portray the representation of an older person. It may also be useful to study the trailer or key scenes from the film to use as further examples.

Film stills from Gran Torino, director Clint Eastwood, Warner Bros (2008)

Representations of events in the media today

The representation of **events** is one of the areas you will need to cover in your preparation for the MS1 examination. For events, the expectation is that you will explore the representation of two events, focussing on two examples from different media texts to support your points. This will allow you to demonstrate your understanding of how events are represented across the media. The wording of the question will be 'in the media today', therefore the events you choose to analyse must be contemporary. When studying the representation of events consider:

- The ideology of the text in which the event features. Is it clear what the text you are using thinks about the event? Is there any evidence of opinion or bias in the representation?

- How the event has been presented, referring to, for example, language and mode of address, anchorage, technical, visual and audio codes and the use of images.

- The construction of the representation. The elements that go to make up the final text will have been constructed in a way that real life is not. When we witness an event in real life we do not see it from three different camera angles and in slow motion. This is often the way we view an event as it is presented to us in the media. It is a selected construction and has been edited often to show a particular viewpoint.

- The process of selection. For whatever ends up on the screen or in print, a lot more will have been left out. Someone will have made the decision about what will be included and what to omit. Consider how this might affect how the audience feels about the event.

- That mediation has occurred.

- The focus of the representation. The way in which a media text is mediated encourages the audience to focus upon a particular aspect of the text to push us towards making assumptions and to draw conclusions. For example, our eyes are drawn to the headlines and cover lines in newspapers and magazines.

- The role of opinion leaders in influencing the audience about the event.

- The audience who will **consume** the text and their response to the representations encoded within it.

Key Terms

Event = An event is something that occurs or is about to occur and is of interest to an audience. Events come in a range of shapes and forms and can be local, national or international. For example, the Royal Wedding, the Olympic Games or a pop festival. International events may include wars and global recession. A local event may the local football team being promoted.

Consume = This is another way of saying how an audience uses a media text. We are all consumers of different media texts.

quickfire

(22) How might opinion leaders affect the way in which an audience may respond to an event as represented in a media text?

Consider how these two texts have represented this event

- *Hello* magazine's target audience like gossip about up-market celebrities. Here, the images selected for the front page show snapshots of the wedding day including 'A' list celebrities like Victoria Beckham. The images suggest the importance of the event.

- The main image has been chosen as the mode of address is direct seeming to engage the *Hello* audience.

- The magazine is a 'souvenir issue' further defining the event as one that will be documented for future audiences.

- The magazine also uses enigma codes to suggest that it has exclusive information and more intimate details about the royal couple to encourage readers to buy the magazine.

- *The Daily Star* is targeting a different audience. Here the event is represented in terms of national pride and **ethnocentricity**.

- The lexis used further emphasises the sense of what it is to be British (according to *The Star*): 'passion, pomp and ceremony'.

- The language used is informal and addresses the reader directly, making them feel part of the event.

- The image of the kiss was one used by many newspapers that day to represent the event and the royal couple.

Key Terms

Ethnocentricity = This is the belief in the superiority of the nation to which we belong, for example Britain. Some newspapers are essentially ethnocentric in that they carry very little foreign news and with regard to an event such as this, will celebrate the greatness of Britain as a nation.

Examiner tip

Consider how these texts could also be used to answer a question on the representation of national identity.

quickfire

㉓ How does the construction of these texts suggest an audience should respond to this event?

The Royal Wedding in April 2011 was a huge national and international event covered by a range of media texts.

Copyright Express Newspapers

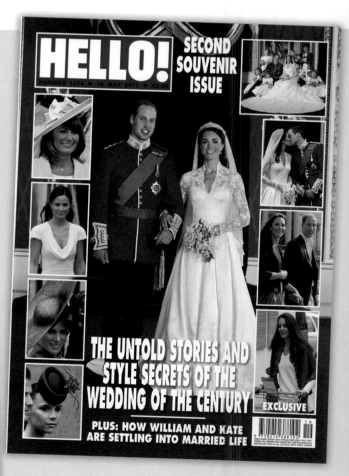

Copyright Hola, SL

Representations of issues in the media today

As well as representing groups in society, the media also construct representations of issues and indeed may be partly responsible for creating the issue itself. This may be the case with the issue of body image in the media. We have become a society obsessed with how we look and what constitutes beauty. The definition of what it is to be beautiful has narrowed and focusses, in the media, almost solely on being white, thin and perfectly formed. This also links to the way in which women in general are represented. The issue of body image in the media is represented across a range of media texts including:

- Unrealistic images of perfection for both men and women in magazines.

- Gossip magazines where imperfections in the bodies of celebrities are highlighted for discussion and ridicule.

- Documentaries raising awareness of the issue.

- Newspaper images of catwalk models that are a size zero.

- Media articles commenting on the concern of the beauty cult that means that only thin is beautiful.

- Images that challenge this representation but that tend to be **tokenistic**.

- Advertisements for products that aim to make the user more beautiful, less wrinkled and flawless. However, these images are unrealistic and have frequently been digitally enhanced. MP Jo Swinson succeeded in getting two beauty adverts banned for including images that were over airbrushed and significantly digitally manipulated. The advertisements for *Lancôme* and *Maybelline* featuring Julia Roberts and Christy Turlington were deemed unacceptable by the ASA as they did not offer a realistic representation of what the product could achieve when used.

- Many advertisements now, often in small print, must declare if the image has been enhanced with implants or hair extensions and post-production.

MatildaInozemceva/Shutterstock.com

Valua Vitaly/Shutterstock.com

Key Term

Tokenism = This is where a media text includes a few members of a minority group, for example some plus size models in a glamour magazine. This appears to redress the balance but in fact, as the group is in the minority they have no real power within the text and their 'difference' from the norm is also highlighted. Tokenism also tends to present a stereotypical view of that group so that audiences can recognise them easily.

Examiner tip

If a question on the representation of issues in the media today appears on the examination paper, it will be for Question 2c or 3. The expectation is that you will have studied two issues and be able to discuss how they were represented across two different media texts. It is important that you are aware of how the issue can be represented differently according to the particular text.

Grade boost

For an MS1 question on issues it is important that you remember to analyse *how* the representation is constructed and presented to an audience as a version of reality. Consider how the images and anchors work together in *Heat* magazine to offer a representation of body image.

Examiner tip

Although we have looked at these examples for representation of issues, consider how you could use them to discuss audience responses to the issues and to the way in which it is presented in these texts.

quickfire

(24) Consider how texts construct the representation of an issue. Use examples to back up your points.

Body image as an issue is represented across a range of media texts targeted at different audiences. How the image is represented depends on the type of text and its potential audience. In magazines women are sold an idealised version of themselves and aspire to attain the unattainable. Many television programmes tackle the issue of body image from a range of points of view. This may be through consideration of weight, plastic surgery or general dissatisfaction with body size. It is generally the case that most of these programmes focus on and are targeted at women.

In *Cherry's Body Dilemmas* (www.bbc.co.uk/programmes/b013y2b1) Cherry Healey confronts her own body obsessions and explores the issue of body image across a range of women. The programme's genre is documentary and includes voice-overs, interviews and fly on the wall filming exposing the insecurities of a range of women regarding how they feel society wants them to look.

This front cover of *Heat* magazine, renowned for its continued focus on the body image of celebrities, effectively demonstrates the concept of the male gaze. The women are judged by men, the suggestion being that it is men who look at them and therefore their attention to their body image should be for men. The front cover focuses upon the perceived imperfections of women in terms of their weight and appearance. The rhetorical questioning encourages women to be unhappy if they have similar body issues to the celebrities featured but also to take heart that even celebrities have these problems.

Heat, *Bauer Consumer Media Ltd*

Representations of gender in the media today

Women

The representation of women in the media has developed and adapted to reflect cultural and sociological changes. As women's roles in society have undergone a transformation, this has been reflected in some areas of the media. However, there are still some stereotypical representations of women where they are defined by how men see them and how society expects them to look and behave. Women still tend to be judged on their looks and appearance foremost. Representations tend to concentrate also on their sexuality; emotions and narratives tend to be based around relationships. The way in which the representation of women is constructed in texts like glamour magazines is unrealistic and instils unattainable aspiration in the audience. In an examination response it is important that you explore the representation of gender at a sophisticated level and go beyond a basic discussion of positive and negative, it is much more complex than that.

The representation of Fearne Cotton as the cover image appeals to both men and women; in simple terms women want to be her, men want to be with her. The cover line related to her defines her very much in terms of a relationship and of emotions: 'being in love'. The image is constructed through visual codes, clothing and mode of address. The image is ambiguous; her posture and body language are strong but she is also very sexualised. She is defined in terms of her body image and her size. By highlighting her 'firm thighs' the magazine presents this representation as that which every woman should aspire to. The other cover lines suggest the discourse of the magazine and represent women in terms of beauty, sex and consumerism. The sell line of 'miracle beauty buys' gives hope to those readers who do not look like the female construction of the magazine. The representation is obviously unrealistic and the construction includes airbrushing to give a representation of perfection – unattainable for most 'ordinary' women.

> **Grade boost**
>
> When discussing areas of representation like, for example, stereotyping, you must ensure that you analyse the representation according to the context in which it appears and the purpose.

> **Examiner tip**
>
> This example can also be used for an audience question. Consider how different audiences might respond to this front cover and what would affect their response, for example their age.

> **Key figure**
>
> Laura Mulvey is a feminist film theorist whose work on the sexual objectification of women through 'the male gaze' can be used to analyse a range of media texts.

Cosmopolitan © Hearst Magazines UK

Whilst there remain many stereotypical representations of women in the media, there are also texts that are constructed to challenge these representations. These texts hold messages that offer a more realistic or refreshing representation of women in the media today. In film and television we see more women who have key roles and who are active rather than passive. They are defined by what they do, rather than what they have done to them. They are less the victim and more the hero.

GHD Twisted Fairy Tales advertising campaign. Courtesy of ghd and Tim Bret Day

Some texts cleverly play with accepted stereotypes in order to challenge them. This is true of the GHD Straighteners *Twisted Fairytales* advertising campaign. Here the **stereotypical** representations of women in fairy tales are **subverted** to create strong women who do not have to rely on men to rescue them. The campaign uses Rapunzel, Cinderella and Red Riding Hood – in each case they leave the stereotypical male hero behind in the 'twist' at the end. In the TV advert, Rapunzel makes her escape on the hero's motorcycle wearing a leather jacket over her traditional 'princess' attire thus further challenging the stereotypical role of the damsel in distress.

In the print advertisement above, Red Riding Hood is both sexually attractive and purposeful. She engages in a direct mode of address with the audience. The iconography and graphics remain that of the fairy tale, but the representation of Red Riding Hood is very different as the rhyme indicates.

However, it is also true that, although the women are strong and independent and overcome the men, they are also stereotypically beautiful and it is their beauty aid, the straighteners that are deemed responsible for their success. In this respect the representation of women in the campaign is ambiguous.

Men

Stereotypically, men in media texts are represented differently from women but their representation, like that of women, has changed in order to address changes in society. There have been many cries that **masculinity** is in crisis and that men no longer have a traditional role to play in society as they once did. However, it is the case that men, just like women, have had to change their roles and this has been reflected in their representation across a range of media texts. With the advent of the **'new man'** there appeared different representations of masculinity. However, even when disguised as a new man, representations of men in the media tend to still focus on:

- Body image and physique
- Physical strength
- Sexual attractiveness and relationships with women
- Power and independence.

One media area that has developed dramatically is the men's magazines market. Now men, as well as women, are given aspirational and unrealistic role models to emulate. Men, too, have to be concerned about their weight and body image and buy into an unattainable lifestyle through the representations presented to them.

Men's Health magazine is now the best selling men's magazine, overtaking *FHM* in 2010. Here we have a constructed representation that defines men very clearly. The central image in one of perfection and has clearly been manipulated to present the 'perfect body' image. The mode of address is direct and the use of imperatives is commanding and powerful. However, as this is a 'new man', he is also concerned about health and diet, but reverts to a more traditional type referring to 'sex' rather than relationships. The cover lines include quick fix problem solving to suggest that achieving a healthy lifestyle and this body is easy. The body language of the model suggests that he is proud of his shape and is self obsessed, looking away from the audience.

Key Terms

Masculinity = This is the state of 'being a man' and this can change as society changes. It is essentially what being a man means to a particular generation. This is then reflected in media texts.

New man = This was a term introduced to describe a new breed of men. These men rejected sexist attitudes; were in touch with their feminine side and were therefore not afraid to be sensitive and caring and could sometimes be seen in a domestic role. A good example of a media text that reflects this changing role is the way in which James Bond's representation has changed to become more acceptable.

Key figure

David Gauntlett is Professor of Media and Communications at the University of Westminster. In his book *Media, Gender and Identity* and his website theory.org.uk he considers the changing representations of men and women in the media.

Men's Health © *Hearst Magazines UK*

Grade boost

It is important that when you are discussing representations in an examination response, you are aware that the representation and the audience response to it will change according to the context.

Grade boost

Try to explore the complexity of the text and do not confine your analysis to basic discussions of positive and negative.

Examiner tip

Consider how one text can be used to comment on more than one area of representation. For example, the *Lynx Excite* television advertisement also includes representations of national identity as the setting is an old Italian town.

Examiner tip

The examples you use in the examination need not be long texts. A film poster or a front cover of a magazine are useful examples as they are rich texts and manageable to discuss in the confines of the examination when you do not have much time.

However, there still exist in the media the more stereotypical representations of men in strong roles defined by their power, independence and their ability to survive against all the odds. These representations tend to be associated with particular genres, for example the action film, still largely the domain of the male protagonist.

Stills from Casino Royale,
director Martin Campbell, MGM (2006)

Quantum of Solace,
director Marc Foster, MGM (2008)

In *Casino Royale* and *Quantum of Solace*, the audience is presented with James Bond, the action hero. The iconography that places him in this role is evident in these stills from the film: the dinner suit, the gun, the action shot and the beautiful woman. However, on closer analysis, this representation is more ambiguous and reflects the 'new man' that is Bond. The woman is not an accessory; she is next to him and has clearly been a part of the action. His bow tie is missing and his suit is slightly dishevelled. His code of expression is not the usual cool and calm, but moody and unhappy. In another shot he is seen as protecting the female and looking intimidated himself.

In the *Lynx Excite* television advertising campaign *Even Angels Will Fall* the 'hero' challenges the traditional stereotype of the 'buff', confident man. He is confused by the attention of the beautiful fallen angels. In this advert a different stereotype is constructed, that of the slightly geeky, weedy young man who will be recognisable to the target audience. The purpose of the representation is to amuse the audience through the unbelievable and enviable situation. This stereotype appears in other media texts, for example *The Inbetweeners* and *Fresh Meat*.

Representations of ethnicity in the media today

Just as with other areas of representation, in the MS1 examination the expectation would be that you would offer an overview demonstrating your understanding of this particular area of representation and then back up your points with examples across a range of media texts (at least three are required). Consider the following general points in relation to the representation of **ethnicity** in the media today:

- The representation of people from other cultures in the media has changed dramatically since earlier days where they were defined in terms of their potential for comedy and their 'foreignness'.

- However, people from other cultures still tend to be defined by their differences and their 'otherness'. This can be used to offer both positive and negative representations of ethnicity in the media.

- Just like other groups within the media, there are stereotypical representations of ethnicity defined generally by **racial** characteristics.

- Stereotypes and mis-representation are even more dangerous when dealing with ethnicity compared to gender, as the representation that is constructed through the media is often the only experience of these cultures that some audiences will encounter.

- People from different ethnic backgrounds are often represented as being exotic in some media texts, for example magazines.

- Young black people have been demonised by some areas of the media and are presented as linked to violence and gang culture in news programmes and some films.

- Tokenism often occurs with regard to the representation of ethnic minorities. For example, the introduction of a British Asian family in a soap opera often means that the storylines will focus around stereotypical aspects of that culture, for example arranged marriages. *EastEnders* does not offer a true representation of the ethnic mix that would exist in that area of London in modern multi-cultural Britain.

- There has been criticism of some programmes, for example *Midsomer Murders,* for their lack of representation of ethnic groups.

- Ethnic minorities are presented more positively in the music industry where there is more scope to celebrate their cultural roots. Rap music's increasing popularity has changed the perceptions of young white people to different ethnic cultures.

Key Terms

Ethnicity = Many people confuse ethnicity and race. Your ethnicity is defined by your cultural identity which may demonstrate itself through customs, dress, food, for example. Ethnicity suggests an identity that is based on a sense of place, ideology or religion. You can be British but of Jewish ethnicity.

Race = Your race is defined by the fact that you descend from a common ancestor giving you a clear set of racial characteristics. That may be related to the colour of your skin and facial features, for example.

25 How are ethnic groups represented in the music industry? Back up your points with specific examples.

Grade boost

Look at the *Newsnight* interview on YouTube. Consider how youth and ethnicity are represented by the guests on the programme and how the sequence has been constructed through technical codes and editing.

Examiner tip

Consider how you could use these examples to also discuss the representation of young people in the media today and to look at the representation of an event. Remember that 'rich' texts are those that can be used for more than one area of the examination paper.

Task

Look at the newspaper pages on page 48 and consider how the riots as an event were represented in the media.

Task

Now find an example of a positive representation of ethnicity in the media today so that you can offer a balanced viewpoint and range of examples in your response.

One of the key events of 2011 was the riots in August and the media response to those riots. The catalyst for the rioting was the shooting dead of 29-year-old black man Mark Duggan on 4 August 2011. He was about to be arrested in association with gun crime in the black community. The newspapers from one day are available to see in another section of this book.

Consider how *The Sun* newspaper represented the man on 5 August before any information was available about the details of what had actually happened. The use of the term 'gangsta' reinforces the ethnicity of the man in a negative way. This is further anchored by the choice of image used with the iconography of 'bling' and the aggressive code of gesture and direct mode of address. This makes links to his ethnic and cultural ideology.

A further, different text is the *Newsnight* interview with David Starkey that is available to watch on YouTube (www.youtube.com/watch?v=OVq2bs8M9HM). This interview is a further example of how the ethnicity was represented, this time on a television programme. David Starkey, a historian, stated about the riots that: 'whites have become blacks', seeming to equate the ethnicity of black youths with criminality and gang culture. After the programme Twitter erupted and there were 700 complaints about his remarks. David Starkey functioned as an opinion leader and the interesting aspect of this particular event was that because of the sporadic and unpredictable nature of the outbreaks of rioting, the opinion leaders became community leaders, Twitter users and ordinary members of the public as they were witnessing events as they happened and interpreting them for the news audience.

Still taken from YouTube - Newsnight, 12/08/11, BBC2

Representations of national and regional identity in the media today

The way in which nations and specific regions are represented in the media today is another area of representation that may appear on the examination paper. This will be an and/or question and your response must be supported by specific examples from three media texts. Representations of **national identity** are reinforced and embedded in our culture. Our own national identity is often defined by our difference in relation to other nations. Our perception of other nations is often of stereotypical character traits, for example 'the French are good cooks', 'the Italians are romantic and emotional'. Sporting events, in particular, tend to show representations of national identity more obviously.

The Rugby World Cup was held in New Zealand in 2011. The trailer for this sporting event is a good example to use for representations of national identity. The trailer combines images representing New Zealand with representations of other nations.

Stills taken from YouTube – Rugby World Cup 2011 Trailer – New Zealand

Key Term

National identity = The representation of a country as a whole, encompassing its culture, traditions, language, and politics. This includes the characteristics of the country that are clearly definable to other nations.

Examiner tip

Sporting events are useful texts to use as examples of national identity. Here you will see examples of nations clearly defined by iconography.

Examiner tip

Consider how this trailer and other similar examples can also be used to explore representations of gender and events.

Grade boost

Remember to demonstrate your understanding of the concept of national identity and how it is represented in media texts before you analyse your examples.

How is national identity represented in this trailer?

- The trailer is constructed and edited to show different representations of national identity.

- Nations are represented by their flags and their strips. These become iconic and carry connotations of hope and pride. In the trailer there are shots of fans with faces painted in the national colours. In the screenshot above, the Welsh dragon is clearly in evidence.

- The supporters are represented as emotional and proud of their national identity. Close-ups of gestures of triumph and facial expressions are shown to reflect this.

- The tag line for the trailer is 'Be There for the Glory', again reinforcing national pride.

- The representation of New Zealand is more varied as they were the host nation. The trailer features shots of its monuments and natural beauty including mountains, oceans and wildlife. This is combined with shots of the Haka representing it as a powerful nation with a strong cultural identity. The aim of the Haka is to reinforce the Maori culture and to intimidate opponents. It is a recognisable feature of New Zealand rugby.

Key Terms

Regional identity = The way in which a particular area of a country is defined by the accent, dialect, dress and customs of its inhabitants.

Accent = The way in which the inhabitants of a particular region speak. For, example, the Scouse accent belongs to those who live or originate from Liverpool.

Dialect = The particular words that have their origins in a specific region and are used by the inhabitants of that region and may be unknown to others. For example, people who live in the North East of England call young children 'bairns'.

Examiner tip

This text is also a useful one to explore representations of issues including poverty, social deprivation and the North–South divide.

Similarly to national identity, the representations of regions as they appear in media texts tend to be defined by characteristics that are recognised by those who are outside of that region. The representation is built up through repetition over time and may focus upon **accent, dialect** and customs in its construction. Again, as for national identity, the representation may be stereotypical and concentrate on accentuated features of that region. For example, the representation of 'Essex girls' in news articles and television comedy programmes plays upon exaggerated references to accent, clothing and lack of intelligence.

In the BBC3 programme, *Geordie Finishing School For Girls*, two regional representations come together as four privileged girls from the South go to Newcastle to experience life on benefits. The programme begins by showing a montage of iconic shots of Newcastle and images of drunken Geordies. The voice-over anchors the images and gives a representation of the region as socially deprived. This is reinforced in the character profiles from the website which contrasts with the 'Chelsea set' that are also defined in terms of stereotypical traits and their narrow-minded intolerance. 'Southern Girl' Fiona Culley states: '*you shouldn't be able to make more money sat on the sofa doing bugger all than you can working, that's where the whole system is screwed*'. 'Geordie', Lyndsey Balfour is described on the website: '*in her teens she drank heavily and made trouble. Now she's turned things around and is a youth worker helping kids with problems.*'

The region is represented through constructed images and edited scenarios as socially deprived and the Geordie girls are defined by their dialect, their chav clothing and their accents. In one scene, the Southern girls are given a lesson in the Geordie dialect. The voice-over continues to act as an anchor to the images and a narrator, helping to build the regional representation. The images on the website are constructed – Geordie girl Lyndsey has a council estate as her background, whereas Fiona is softly lit and framed by a more pleasant background thus reinforcing difference.

Stills taken from YouTube – Geordie Finishing School for Girls, BBC3

Summary: Representation for MS1

- 'Representation' may be the topic for either Question 2c or Question 3.

- Remember to check the word allocation – Question 3 is worth more marks and therefore you must write more.

- You must ensure that you have examples from the following areas of representation:
  - Gender
  - Ethnicity
  - Age
  - Issues
  - Events
  - Regional and national identities.

- Remember, if you use examples of **rich texts** then one text can be used for more than one area of representation and may also be used for the audience question.

- When answering a question on gender, age, ethnicity or regional/national identities you will be expected to support your discussion with three examples of different media texts. If you choose three similar texts, for example three magazines, you will end up saying the same thing three times.

- These examples must be as specific as possible. For example, do not just refer to 'women in magazines', but comment on a particular front cover. If you are using a moving image example then select a particular scene that will best support what you want to say about representation. This will help you to avoid producing a general response.

- The question will ask you about representations 'in the media **today**' therefore your examples must be contemporary, although you may want to refer to an older example briefly to illustrate a point.

- Structure your response in a logical and coherent manner. Try to start with an introductory paragraph demonstrating your understanding of the concept of representation.

- As part of your revision, plan which examples of media texts you have studied in class will best answer the different areas of representation.

- Read the question carefully and answer it. Remember to refer back to the question where you can in your response. Do not answer the question you wish had been asked!

- Make sure that your examples are relevant to the question.

Key Term

Rich texts = These are texts that you could use for more than one area of the specification. For example, the trailer and key scenes from *Slumdog Millionaire* can be used to discuss representations of national identity, age, gender and the issue of poverty as well as being a useful text to use when analysing audience responses and targeting.

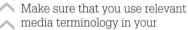

Grade boost

Make sure that you use relevant media terminology in your response and that you analyse the examples you have chosen – avoid describing them.

MS1

Audience

In the MS1 examination, audience may be the focus for either Question 2c or Question 3. You will need to consider:

- The ways in which audiences can be categorised and described. This may change according to the industry. For example, the advertising industry describes audiences differently and more specifically than other media industries.

- The ways in which audiences and users are constructed by media texts and the response an audience may have to that construction.

- The ways in which media texts position audiences. This may be to involve the audience or to elicit a response.

- The ways in which different audiences and users respond to, use and interpret different texts.

- The ways in which media texts target and appeal to audiences. This will also come from an understanding that all media industries operate in a competitive market and must ensure that they market to the audience effectively.

Understanding audiences: key points

- The relationship between the media text and the audience is fluent and changing.

- Unlike in the past, there is no longer assumed to be only one way of interpreting a text and only one audience response.

- Audiences are not mass and their responses are complex and sophisticated and are influenced by a range of factors.

- The audience are made up of individuals whose social and cultural experiences may affect how they respond to any media text.

- Media texts and the industries that produce them are acutely aware of their audience and the strategies needed to attract them.

- There are a range of theories that explain the different ways in which audiences respond to media texts and the reasons for this.

Audience positioning

Media texts are constructed in order to place audiences in a particular position in relation to that text. Audience positioning concerns the relationship between the text and the responses an audience may have to that text. The producers of the texts encode the texts with signs and messages and the audience decode these messages. Different audiences will decode the same texts in different ways and will therefore have a different response. In Question 2c or 3 of the MS1 examination you may be asked to discuss how media texts position audiences. You must support your points with specific examples.

How do media texts position audiences?

- Through the technical codes employed by the text. In a moving image text, the camera shots and angles used place the audience in a particular position. For example, the use of a close-up shot at an emotional time in the narrative may encourage the audience to be sympathetic to the character. A point of view shot positions the audience as a character and allows them to experience events from that perspective. This may enhance the audience pleasure in the text. However, the positioning may be an uncomfortable one. For example, the use of an extreme close-up of a character's face in a tense moment may make the audience feel uncomfortable. The camera may take the audience where they do not want to go, for example in a horror film.

- Through the language and mode of address. The use of chatty and colloquial language in teenage magazines positions the intended audience as part of the world of the magazine. They make the audience feel involved through the use of a direct and informal mode of address and the use of a specific lexis. The formal language and mode of address used by quality newspapers positions the audience differently. It makes them feel superior and valued as a reader and the expectation is that they will understand and want to be informed.

- Through the construction of the text and of the audience within the text, media texts can be said to construct an idea of their audience or user. The reader of a particular magazine, for example, is 'told' by the magazine what is important and how they should live their lives.

Audience responses to positioning

The positioning of audiences by media texts suggests that the audience should accept the messages contained within the text and decode the text in the way expected by the text's producers. However, as we have stated previously, audiences do not all respond to the same text in the same way. They may accept or challenge the messages encoded within the text. Stuart Hall accepted that **audiences** were **active**, not **passive** and suggested that there were three main ways in which an audience may respond to a media text:

- **Preferred reading** – this is where the audience accepts the dominant reading of the text and interprets the text in the way that the producer of the text intended. This is usually the case if the text reflects the ideas and beliefs of the audience. For example, the readers of *The Daily Mail* will broadly agree with the paper's stance on issues like asylum seekers and young people or they would not read the newspaper. There is, therefore, little for the audience to challenge.

- **Negotiated reading** – this is where the audience accepts some of the text and disagrees with others therefore negotiating over their acceptance of what is presented to them. For example, an audience may buy *Cosmopolitan* magazine for the fashion articles and the interviews but may not accept the sexual content of the text. Or an audience agrees with the press that something must be done about the rioters in August 2011 but does not agree that only young people were to blame.

- **Oppositional reading** – this is where the audience does not agree with the ideology of the text or its content. This may be related to the culture, age, gender or other factors affecting audience response. For example, an older person watching *The Inbetweeners* may have an oppositional reading of the text because of the language, humour and sexual content.

Key Terms

Active audience = This describes an audience who responds to and interprets the media texts in different ways and who actively engages with the messages in the ways suggested here.

Passive audience = This describes an audience that does not engage actively with the text. They are more likely to accept the preferred meaning of the text without challenge. This also suggests that passive audiences are more likely to be directly affected by the messages contained within the text.

Grade boost

Prepare yourself for the examination by considering three specific examples of texts where the audience is positioned in a particular way. Explain how the positioning is achieved. Ensure that your examples are from different media forms.

Key figure

Stuart Hall is a cultural theorist who explored the issue of how people make sense of media texts. He is a proponent of the reception theory and suggested that texts are encoded by the producers of the text and decoded differently by different audiences.

What affects the way in which an audience responds to a media text?

Key Terms

Desensitisation = This is a psychological process that suggests that audiences who are exposed regularly to acts of violence through films and video games, for example, are increasingly less likely to feel empathy or concern when exposed to violence, bad language or other forms of aggressive behaviour.

Cultural competence = Within a media context, this idea suggests that the cultural competence of an audience is the shared knowledge, related to their cultural understanding, of that audience, which means that they will take a particular pleasure from a media text. For example, the audience who understand and engage with the rules of *Call of Duty*, and have a certain computer literacy, will enjoy the control aspect of the game and the online sharing of techniques.

quickfire

(26) Using the texts you have studied in class, explain how gender or age may affect responses to those texts. Be specific in your response.

Task

Watch the trailer for the film *Sherlock Holmes* starring Jude Law and Robert Downey Jnr. How might different audiences respond to this text?

As we said earlier, an audience is not a mass all behaving the same way; it is made up of individuals who, according to a range of factors, will respond to the same media text in different ways. This may be related to:

- Gender – different genders respond to different media texts differently. It has been suggested, for example, that women enjoy the themes and narratives of television programmes like soap operas more than men. This may be because they deal with relationships and domestic narratives which are in the experiences of most women. They can therefore empathise with the characters and their situation. However, it is important to avoid simple generalisations; many men also watch these genres of programmes.

- Age – again, we need to be careful of making generalisations, but different ages will respond differently to media texts. Older audiences may be less comfortable with sexually explicit texts with a high level of bad language. However, a younger audience, who have been more **desensitised** to this sort of content, will be more comfortable consuming this type of text.

- Ethnicity – ethnic groups from different cultural backgrounds may respond to texts differently because of their ideas, beliefs and upbringing. For example, the film *Four Lions*, a comedy based around suicide bombers, may elicit different responses according to the ethnic makeup of the audience. Different ethnic groups may also have strong responses to how they themselves are represented in media texts.

- Culture and cultural experience – the culture, upbringing and experiences of the audience will often shape their view of and response to media texts. Media texts also shape our experience and manipulate our responses to other texts. For example, we may have never been in hospital but our experience of hospitals has been formed from television programmes. The audience then feel in a position to challenge or comment on procedures in one media text from their experience of viewing a different text. The experience will not be actual.

- **Cultural competence** – this may also relate to age and gender and is developed over time. Some audiences have different 'cultural competencies' to others, this is particularly true with regard to users of the Internet and video games, where understanding is shared amongst those who 'use' the texts. The playing of video games tends to be within the cultural competence of young men. Women tend to not know 'what is going on' in these types of texts and are therefore alienated as it is outside of their cultural competence. Likewise the use of computer terminology.

- Situated culture – this concerns the 'situation' of the audience and how that may affect how they respond to a media text. This may mean literally where the audience is. The communal viewing of a film in a cinema, in the dark, produces a very different response and pleasure compared to watching the same film in a well-lit sitting room where you may be interrupted and distracted. Who you watch the text with will affect response. For example, watching *The Inbetweeners* with an older person in the room may produce a more uncomfortable viewing experience for a teenager.

Audience theories: relevant theoretical frameworks

There are several theories that have been written about audiences, how texts appeal to them and how and why they respond in different ways. It may be helpful when answering some of the questions that may be set in the MS1 examination to refer to theories and demonstrate your understanding of them in relation to your textual examples. The most useful theoretical frameworks at MS1 are as follows.

The uses and gratifications theory

This theory was developed as a response to other outdated theories, for example the **hypodermic needle effect**. This was one of the first theories to suggest that audiences were not a mass unit and were not all passive. The suggestion is that active audiences seek out and use different media texts in order to satisfy a need and to experience different pleasures including:

- **For entertainment and diversion** – audiences consume some media texts in order to escape from the mundanity and pressures of everyday life. This also suggests that audiences do not have to experience literal reality but can become equally involved in a story world that is believably fantastical if it offers escapism. For example, for the length of the film, an audience can escape into the seemingly believable world of *Harry Potter* and Hogwarts School as the reality of that world is so well constructed through technical codes, characters and narrative.

- **For information and education** – some texts are consumed by audiences when they want to know what is going on in the world or to find out information about other areas of the world. For example, the appeal of BBC 1's *Frozen Planet* is that is gives its audience access to parts of the world they are highly unlikely to visit themselves. News programmes and newspapers keep audiences informed about current affairs. Magazines with a niche audience also contain information relevant to a particular area, for example *Jump* magazine and the *Urban Freeflow* website keep readers up to date with the world of parkour and free-running.

- **For social interaction** – some media texts are 'of the moment' and are discussed by the audience as they happen. This is sometimes referred to as **'water-cooler' television**. Audiences watch the programme or film or play the latest video game so that they can then use the experience to talk to others. An example would be *The X-Factor* where, the next day, audiences discuss the relative merits of the contestants, the judges and who should win. Here, the audience response is immediate and to be involved, it is essential to keep up to date with the programme.

- **For personal identity** – this is the idea that audiences will gain pleasure from some media texts because they are able to compare their lives and circumstances with those featured in the particular text. An example would be soap operas including *Hollyoaks* and *EastEnders*, where narratives tend to focus on relationships and social issues. The appeal of the programme may be that an audience can empathise with a particular character in a situation and be involved with how they handle it. This is also true with respect to some lifestyle magazines that feature 'real-life stories' where audiences can identify personally with the situation described.

Key Term

Opinion leaders = Those people in society who may affect the way in which an audience interprets the media. For example, politicians, teachers, celebrities and parents.

Key figure

Paul Lazarsfeld. In 1940 he conducted research into the Presidential election campaign and discovered that social influences, rather than the media, had a major effect upon how voters would respond. This led to the development of the two-step flow response theory.

David Gauntlett's 'pick and mix' theory

This is another theory that understands the autonomy of the audience. It counteracts the theory that all audiences are affected by what they read. Gauntlett focuses on the way in which magazines and advertisements attract and represent audiences. His suggestion is that audiences are sophisticated and use texts to satisfy their needs. They pick the bits of the text that are appropriate to them and their lives and ignore the others. This challenges the theory that women, for example, will be adversely affected by the unrealistic images they see on the front covers of women's magazines. They may read the magazine, ignoring the articles related to sex and relationships and 'pick' the articles on fashion and beauty.

Two-step flow and opinion leaders

This response/effects theory was another to challenge the hypodermic needle model and the notion of the media transmitting a message that was then absorbed in the same way by a mass audience. This theory suggests that there are other factors at play that will affect the way in which an audience responds to media messages encoded within texts. The findings of the research conducted in 1940 by Lazarsfeld and others suggested that the ideas and opinions of other people affected how an audience may respond to the media. This may be conversations with friends, the opinions of experts and their own cultural experiences and upbringing. The people who may affect the way in which an audience responds to a media text are called **opinion leaders**. These may be politicians, celebrities, friends or parents, whose interpretation of the media may be listened to and trusted by the audience. However, it is also the case that we, as an audience, may not respond actively to the opinion leaders.

The audience may not have even seen the actual media text themselves, hence the 'two-step flow' but may be influenced by the opinion leader. For example, the reviews in newspapers by recognised film critics and similar quotes on film posters will influence an audience who have yet to see the film in question. This is particularly true if they trust and value the opinions of those commenting on the text. Politicians commenting on a newspaper story may influence an audience's response to that story without them having read it themselves.

This theory also reinforces the idea that audiences are sophisticated in their responses, are individuals and are active, not passive.

How audiences are constructed by media texts

The idea that media texts themselves construct a notion of their audience is a more complex approach to the study of media texts. Certain texts can be said to construct an idea of their audience. This can be achieved through the images, content and representations included within the text. Some texts, for example magazines, will produce **media or press packs** for advertisers, containing information about their audience. Some of this will be from audience research but some will be an idea of who that audience is and who the text would like them to be. There is often a difference between the text's construction of the audience and the actual consumer of the product.

For example, take the case of men's and women's magazines. Magazines like *Men's Health* and *Cosmopolitan* will construct the audience of their magazine through the front cover, the content and the language and mode of address. They therefore create assumptions about the lifestyle of the audience and establish what is 'normal' in the world of the magazine. These magazines, for audiences, tend to be aspirational and as such do not reflect the true lifestyle of the consumer.

'Cosmopolitan is the lifestylist and cheerleader – for millions of fun, fearless females who want to be the best they can be in every area of their lives.' Cosmopolitan website.

This assertion is backed up by the January 2012 issue of the magazine which sells its readers a particular lifestyle. The expectation is that they have a glamorous party life, the cover lines focus on '*329 dance floor-rocking party looks*' and that they are in a sexual relationship. The reader is also a career woman '*Get That Job! Unleash your secret career weapon!*' the cover image is of American actress Katherine Heigl dressed for a party with a perfect body, looks and a winning smile!

Audience categories

Different media industries categorise audiences in order to define them easily and to consider how they can be targeted. The magazine and advertising industries, in particular, tend to still categorise audiences in terms of income, lifestyle and needs, although this is seen to be an outdated method of classifying an audience. It may still be used because these industries are focussing on selling a clearly defined product and they must therefore be accurate about the target audience. Audiences can be defined through their **demographic profile** or through their psychometric profile:

- **A demographic audience profile** categorises an audience from A to E according to their class, occupation and income, where categories A and B are the wealthiest and most influential members of society and are therefore assumed to have the most disposable income. It is used by advertisers to determine where advertisements should be placed according to the demographic profile of the audience. Some media texts will use the demographic profiling to inform advertisers of the target audience. In their Press Pack *Men's Health* magazine claims: '*We reach more AB 25–44-year-old men than GQ and Esquire added together*'.

- Interestingly, retired people used to be in category E to reflect their loss of income, but with the rise of early retirement with a lucrative pension and the '**silver surfer**', this group has moved to a higher category to reflect their disposable income and their obvious appeal to advertisers.

Key Terms

Magazine press/media pack = This is put together by the owners of magazines and is intended to give information to advertisers. It informs them about the details of the assumed target audience including income, marital status and age. It usually gives a pen portrait of the audience. The pack also includes the rates to place an advertisement in the magazine. However, they are also a useful resource for media students and can be downloaded or requested from the magazine.

Demographic profiling = Dividing consumers into groups based on age, sex, income, education, occupation, household size, marital status, home ownership or other factors. This information can help advertisers determine their target audience for particular products and develop adverts that focus on a specific demographic.

Silver surfer = This is an older person who is computer literate and uses the net to purchase goods and find out information.

quickfire

28 Using Stuart Hall's response theory, suggest how different audiences may respond to *Cosmopolitan* magazine.

Examiner tip

This type of audience categorisation is specific to certain media industries, for example advertising and magazines. Be careful of trying to categorise audiences of other media texts in the same way.

- Age and gender are also aspects of demographic profiling and some texts, as seen in the *Men's Health* example below, will publish details of their target audience in order to provide broad information for the advertisers.

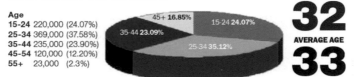

How old are our readers?

Age
15-24 220,000 (24.07%)
25-34 369,000 (37.58%)
35-44 235,000 (23.90%)
45-54 120,000 (12.20%)
55+ 23,000 (2.3%)

MEDIAN AGE
32
AVERAGE AGE
33

45+ 16.85%
15-24 24.07%
35-44 23.09%
25-34 35.12%

Men's Health Media Pack, Hearst Magazines UK

Examiner tip

Again, the Young and Rubicam method of categorising audiences is very useful when analysing advertisements and magazines but is not as useful for other types of media texts.

Examiner tip

Be careful of just downloading this information. Consider why it is important for advertisers to categorise audiences and apply the theory to one of the texts you have studied to illustrate your understanding of audience.

quickfire

㉙ Think of some examples of advertisements whose audience may be categorised using Young and Rubicam's Four Cs.

Key figures

Young and Rubicam are a New York advertising agency who developed a method of categorising people into recognisable stereotypes that reflected their motivational needs.

- **A psychometric audience profile** defines an audience by their values, attitudes and lifestyles (VALs). As the concept of class and income became a less appropriate way of defining an audience, advertisers considered different ways of categorising audiences. One of the most useful to consider when discussing how advertisers define audiences is Young and Rubicam's Four Cs. This advertising agency considered how Cross Cultural Consumer Characteristics can group people into seven recognisable stereotypes reflected through motivational needs and VALs including security, control, status, individuality, freedom, survival and escape. The main groups are:

  – **Mainstreamers** – these make up 40% of the population. They like security, tried and trusted brands and like to think they belong to a group of like-minded people. They like value for money and are less likely to take risks.

  – **Aspirers** – this group want status and prefer brands that show their place in society. They are happy to live on credit and will buy items like designer labels. They are stylish and dynamic and may be persuaded by celebrity endorsement.

  – **Explorers** – like to discover new things. They are attracted by brands that offer new experiences and instant results.

  – **Succeeders** – these are people who already have status and control and have nothing to prove. They prefer brands that are serious and reliable and believe that they deserve the best.

  – **Reformers** – this group are defined by their self-esteem and self-fulfilment. They tend to be innovative and are less impressed by status. They are not materialistic and are socially aware. They may be more inclined to buy brands that are environmentally friendly or those that are considered healthy.

How do media texts target/appeal to audiences?

In the MS1 examination, you may be asked a 'text out' rather that an 'audience in' question. This means that you will have to consider how media texts attempt to attract their audience using examples from a range of texts to support your points. Firstly, it may be useful to consider the target audience of the media text. This will differ according to the type of text; for example, some media texts operate narrow casting and are targeting a niche audience. Other texts will attempt to attract as wide an audience as possible through a range of methods. You will then need to consider how the texts attract their target audience. Methods could include:

- **Technical and audio codes** – the text may employ these to target an audience. The fast-paced editing and dramatic music of a trailer for an action film serves to attract audiences, likewise the bright colours and varied fonts of a gossip magazine.

- **The language and mode of address** may target a specific audience and alienate another. For example, the images and text on the *Call Of Duty* games cover may use lexis and a tone specific to an audience of young men, only they will understand the language and references as they are the intended audience. The voice-over of a horror film may attract fans of the genre by the tone of voice and the promise of a horrific narrative.

- **The construction** of the text and the audience within the text. The way in which, for example, the trailer for a film is edited and constructed will be designed to target an audience. This may involve enigmas, multi-stranded narratives, the use of stars and their roles and the persuasive voice-over. A magazine may, using the image, sell lines and cover lines on its front cover, construct a clear idea of who the audience of the magazine should be.

- **The context** is very relevant – the placing of an advertisement for lager or a sports car aimed at a male audience in the advertising break in a football match, will more obviously target the audience for the product.

- **The positioning of the audience**. This may be through the camera shots and angles, the use of music and other audio codes, the language and mode of address or through empathy with the characters.

> ## ≋ Grade boost
> Include an opening paragraph. This will allow you to demonstrate that you have understood the focus of the question, i.e. targeting. You will also be able to demonstrate an overview understanding of audience in a media context and why texts need to target audiences. This overview is important to allow you to demonstrate a broad understanding of the question and to place it in context.

Everett Collection/Shutterstock.com

Examiner tip

Look for the key word in the question that will help you to focus on the correct area of audience. Make sure that you have two further texts to analyse, showing your broad understanding of the concept.

quickfire

(30) Suggest two further texts you have studied that would be useful in an audience question.

Using examples

Watch the trailer for *Sherlock Holmes a Game of Shadows*. Consider how this text may be used as an example to discuss audience issues for MS1.

Target audience?

- Fans of the stars, Robert Downey Jnr and Jude Law and their previous films.
- Those interested in the original stories of Sherlock Holmes.
- Fans of the director Guy Richie and his other films.
- Those who saw the previous *Sherlock Holmes* film and liked it.
- The action elements of the film may attract some audiences.
- Categories defined by demographic or psychometric profiles.

How is the audience positioned by the text?

- The camera positions us to empathise with Sherlock Holmes and defines the villain clearly to the audience.
- The humour within the film positions the audience as co-conspirators.
- We are encouraged to empathise with Dr Watson's predicament.
- The camera positions the audience as part of the action.

Audience theories

- The uses and gratification theory is useful here as an audience may watch this film for escapism and diversion.
- If they saw the film when it was released then it may have been a subject for social interaction.

Audience responses and what might affect that response

- A younger audience, with no experience of Sherlock Holmes films or stories, may enjoy the Hollywood treatment and the action elements of the film. They will therefore accept the preferred reading of the text intended by the producers.
- A negotiated response may come from an audience who accept the different depiction of Holmes but may not like the Hollywood treatment.
- An oppositional response may come from those sections of the audience who may question the casting of Robert Downey Jnr as the lead role. This audience may also have expected a more traditional treatment of the Sherlock Holmes story, particularly if they are familiar with the older films. This may be an older, more traditional audience.
- The response may also be affected by the gender, situation, ethnicity and cultural competence of the audience.

Summary: Audience for MS1

- 'Audience' may be the topic for either Question 2c or Question 3.

- Remember to check the word allocation – Question 3 is worth more marks than Question 2c and therefore you must write more.

- The areas related to audience that you must prepare for are:
  - Ways of defining and categorising audiences.
  - What affects the way in which audiences respond to media texts.
  - How texts construct audiences.
  - How audiences are positioned by media texts.
  - How media texts attract and appeal to audiences.

- Relevant theoretical frameworks to discuss audiences and audience responses.

- You must support your discussion about audiences by referring to three examples from different media texts. If you choose three similar texts, for example three magazines, you will end up saying the same thing three times.

- These examples must be as specific as possible. For example, do not just refer to 'soap operas', but comment on a particular scene or a character in the programme. If you are referring to a magazine, for example, you should be able to discuss what is on that particular front page. This will help you to avoid producing a general response.

- If you refer to an audience theory, ensure that it is relevant to the example you are discussing.

- Structure your response in a logical and coherent manner. Try to start with an introductory paragraph demonstrating your understanding of the question.

- As part of your revision, plan which examples of media texts you have studied in class will best answer the different aspects of audience.

- Read the question carefully and answer it. Remember to refer back to the question where you can in your response. Do not answer the question you wish had been asked!

Examiner tip

Do not fall into the trap of 'downloading' theories you have learned. If you are using theories, they must be applied to the texts you have chosen to support your points.

Grade boost

Make sure that you use relevant media terminology in your response and that you analyse the examples you have chosen – avoid describing them.

Media Production Process: Approaching MS2

Key Terms

Brief = This will be given to you by your teacher, or you may be asked to come up with one yourself. A brief outlines what you need to do for your internally assessed work and what is expected of you. It may also incorporate deadlines.

Artefact = For the purpose of this unit, this means an actual media text, for example pages of a magazine or a script. It does not mean a series of planning tasks, for example ideas for font styles and mood boards.

Original material = Whatever format you choose to work in, what you produce must be your own work. The majority of images must be taken by you and not downloaded from the Internet, for example. This is the case even if you have engaged in substantial manipulation of the found image. You must bear this in mind in the planning stages of your work.

Comparison with similar products = Ideally, you should aim to produce work that is as professional as you can make it. In your report one of the best ways to evaluate your work is to compare it to a similar text. This may be one of the texts you analysed in your initial research.

Internally assessed work

MS2 is the unit of the AS course that you will complete in your centre and it's then assessed by your teachers. A sample of the work from your centre is then sent to an external moderator whose job it is to ensure that the standard of marking in your centre is the same as it is in other parts of the country.

The MS2 unit is designed to allow you to demonstrate your knowledge and understanding of media texts and to illustrate your skills in: research, production and evaluation. Your teacher will give you a **brief** and guide you through the stages of this unit. This pre-production work may reflect and develop from topics you have studied in class.

What do you need to do for MS2?

You will need to produce **three** pieces of **linked** work:

- **A Pre-production artefact** reflecting your ability to engage in appropriate and relevant research.

- **A Production**: either an audio-visual production or a print production. Print productions must be 2/3 pages of **original material**, audio visual productions must be up to 3 minutes in length.

- **A Report** of a maximum 1600 words. This report should:

  – Outline the research undertaken.

  – Explain how the research has been used to inform the pre-production.

  – Outline and justify the target audience for the production – and explain HOW the audience has been targeted.

  – Evaluate the production, summarising its strengths and weaknesses; preferably by **comparing it with similar products**.

Examples of linked work

Pre-production: the script or storyboard for a new BBC crime drama.

Production: the trailer for the crime drama OR the DVD cover and billboard poster for the programme.

Pre-production: the front cover and contents page of a new magazine aimed at a youth market.

Production: three further front covers in which you develop the house style of the magazine.

Key points to remember

- Your research must be summarised and discussed in your report. You must not submit extra items of research, e.g. mood boards and annotated examples.

- Your pre-production work must be of a high standard. Hand-drawn artefacts are not acceptable. Imagine how it works in the actual industry: if you were submitting your ideas for a front cover of the next issue of a magazine on which you were working, you would not use sketches, you would have produced your ideas and designs on a computer.

- The majority of your images must be original, i.e. produced/taken by you. You must not download images that were not generated by you. You will need to consider this when you make decisions about what you want to create. For example, you can still produce a celebrity gossip magazine, but you must make your friends into new celebrities who can then appear on the front cover with images taken by you!

- Your production piece must be linked to your pre-production in some way. If you make sensible decisions then most pre-production pieces will allow you to choose either an audio-visual or print option.

- Group work is only an option at the production stage if you are working in audio-visual media. Pre-production tasks must be undertaken individually. For group work the group must be a maximum of four and the group members must select one of their pre-productions to develop into a production. Each member of the group must have a clear technical role within the production, for example editing and/or filming. Three is an ideal group size.

- To help when it comes to writing your final report, it may help to make notes on your research and planning for the pre-production before you start your production and while this is still fresh in your mind.

A sample pre-production brief

AS MEDIA STUDIES
MS2 MEDIA PRODUCTION PROCESSES
PRE-PRODUCTION TASKS

You must choose **one** of the following tasks:

- The storyboard for the title and opening sequence of a new crime drama. The storyboard should be in the correct format and should comprise approximately 20 frames.

- The storyboard for the trailer for a new horror/vampire film.

Your aim in creating the storyboard is to convey the overall 'feel' of the programme/film. You should have a clear idea of how the trailer/opening sequence would appear as a moving image.

RESEARCH

You should engage in some of the following **research** in preparation:

- Reading books or studying web pages to develop your understanding of genre conventions, representation, etc.

- Textual analysis – you will need to analyse examples of texts similar to the ones you are to produce considering the generic codes and conventions employed and what you might use.

- If you are producing a storyboard, you need to research the appropriate layout, technical terminology, etc.

- Audience research – you need to consider who your target audience will be and how you will attract them. It may be appropriate to engage in focus group research or to design useful questionnaires.

Key Terms

Sample brief = This is just one way in which the pre-production task may be presented to you in order to guide you through the process. In this example, the students had studied crime dramas and vampire horror films in class during the first term of preparation for MS1.

Research = Just as in the industry, you would never embark upon a new production without first researching other similar products and the target audience. It is important that you engage in research which you will then discuss in your report.

Moderator tip
If you decide to work as part of a group, make sure that you can work well with the rest of the group members and that you have thought carefully about which pre-production piece to take forward into production.

Moderator tip
Be organised! Your teacher will tell you how long you have to complete the work and give you deadline dates. Plan your time carefully remembering to leave plenty of time for editing if you are producing an audio-visual piece.

Moderator tip

One of the best ways to evaluate your own product is to compare it with similar existing products. Remember to be specific.

Moderator tip

If you are working as part of a group producing an audio-visual production piece, ensure that you are clear about your technical role and your responsibilities within the group.

Moderator tip

Your report does not have to be written in continuous prose, it can be illustrated with, for example, screen shots to illustrate points made.

Although this is a pre-production task, your finished pieces should be well presented and demonstrate technical competence. Your texts must show awareness of genre conventions and be appropriate for your suggested target audience.

PRE-PRODUCTION REPORT NOTES (approx. 500–700 words)

This will help you to write your final report after you have completed your production assignment. Your notes should:

- Outline the research you have undertaken explaining how it helped you to produce your pre-production artefact.

- Explain who your target audience is and how your texts have been constructed to appeal to them.

PRODUCTION COURSEWORK

This is the final part of the coursework and must develop out of the pre-production planning. It is worth 40 marks. You must:

- Produce a technically competent media production.

- Evaluate your own production work, which will be incorporated in one report in which you also discuss your pre-production research and artefact.

Print-based productions and interactive media must be produced individually and must contain 2–3 pages of original material. The majority of the images within the production must be original. Audio and audio-visual productions should be 2–3 minutes in length and students can work in groups with clearly defined specific technical roles.

OPTIONS

From the storyboard of a crime drama opening sequence or a vampire/horror film trailer:

- A DVD cover and poster marketing the programme/film.

- A front cover and article in a TV listings/film magazine launching the programme/film.

- A trailer for the crime drama/vampire film.

- The opening sequence/extract from the programme/film.

REPORT (1200–1600 words)

This should include:

- A brief outline of the task.

- A discussion of the most significant research findings which informed the pre-production.

- A brief justification of the target audience for the production.

- An evaluation of the production which highlights it strengths and weaknesses through, for example, a comparison with existing media products.

- Students who have worked as part of a group for audio-visual products will need to evaluate their own individual contribution.

TIPS

- Attempt to develop a sophisticated level of technical capability and creativity to access the higher levels.

- Be original in your ideas and processes.

- Ensure that your finished product is as professional as you can make it with the equipment at your disposal.

Approaching research

Why do you need to conduct research?

You cannot produce a professional and valid piece of pre-production or production work without first researching the area in which you are working. This is particularly true as you do not actually work in the industry, therefore you need to find out as much as you can about the text you want to produce. It is also essential that you research the audience who may consume your particular text in order to discover their opinions. Thorough and useful research will help you to create a better pre-production or production and will allow you to discuss your research findings in detail in your report.

Different types of research

You will need to employ the most appropriate research for the text you have chosen to produce. It is also important that you are clear about what you want to find out by engaging in this research and how it will then help when you produce your own text. **Primary research** is probably the most relevant for the MS2 unit.

Textual analysis

Looking at texts similar to the one you want to create is a useful means of researching generic codes and conventions. It may be that you then decide to replicate or subvert these conventions. Make sure that, in your report, you can refer to specific examples of research you have engaged in. For example, if you were creating a storyboard for the opening sequence of a crime drama, it would be important to research crime dramas from different sub-genres considering characters, setting, narrative and plot situations, representations and technical and audio codes. You then need to give specific examples of the films or television programmes you analysed. It may help to construct a grid to help you to record your findings and to see similarities and differences. You can then decide which features to use in your storyboard – it may be that you focus on establishing the characters in your opening sequence, or introducing narrative strands, or establishing the particular sub-genre, for example forensics.

If you decide to create a magazine front cover and contents page, for example, you may engage in textual analysis focusing on the central image chosen, the style of fonts used, the mode of address, the use of colour and the clues to the magazine's genre. You may also find it helpful to look at the website for the magazines you are analysing where you can research their ethos and ideology. Annotating examples will help you to focus your research and give you specific examples for your report.

Key Term

Primary research = This is information you gain first hand from looking at the actual examples of media texts. Secondary research is found in books and websites, for example, and is written by someone else about the media text you may want to research. It will contain the ideas and opinion of the writer. Primary research allows you to formulate your own opinions.

Moderator tip

It may be the case that you can use some of the texts you have studied in class if your MS2 brief has developed from MS1 work. However, it is still useful to broaden your research and look at examples of your own specific to your chosen sub-genre. This will also help you to produce a more original report.

Audience research

Key Terms

Quantitative research =
This is research that is measurable in numbers and is usually obtained through questionnaires. This type of research will tell you, for example, how many of the people questioned preferred *Waking the Dead* and how many preferred to watch *CSI: Miami*. However, it will not give you the reasons for their decision. Quantitative data is linked to statistics.

Qualitative research =
This method of research gives more information and is more concerned with the 'quality' of the responses rather than the 'quantity'. This type of research is usually obtained through interviews and focus groups.

Focus group = A focus group is a form of qualitative research in which a group of people are asked about their perceptions, opinions, beliefs and attitudes about a product. The aim is to help the producers of the product to ascertain the needs of their target audience.

In the industry a media text would not be produced without first conducting research into the audience who will buy it. The industry employs market research companies to conduct their research for them – you will need to consider ways to find out the opinions of your target audience. **However, audience research must be relevant and useful and will not be an appropriate form of research for all pre-production tasks.**

Audience research can be **quantitative** or **qualitative**. An example of quantitative research is designing a questionnaire. If you choose this method of audience research you need to spend some time constructing a questionnaire that will give you the information you require. Consider:

- Who you are going to ask. Will you give your questionnaire out to a random sample or will you target a specific group? This may depend on the text you intend to produce. If you are producing a storyboard for a film trailer you may want to give out your questionnaires at the local cinema. If you are producing a magazine for 13–15-year-old girls then you may be able to give your questionnaire out in a lesson in your school thus targeting the relevant audience.

- How many people you will survey. The more questionnaires you can distribute the better, this makes your research and data more valid.

- The types of questions you will ask. Avoid questions that give yes/no responses; they will not give you any detailed information. Try to design questions that allow the person to give you more information. This may mean that you need to give them more space to fill in their answers or for you to write down their responses. This is more problematic if you intend to stop people in the street who may not have time to complete this more detailed questionnaire. Designing a questionnaire that is fit for purpose is therefore essential and needs some thought.

- If you are short of time then you could design questions with multiple choice responses.

- How you will use your findings to influence the decisions about your pre-production text and to refer to in your report.

An example of a method of qualitative research is a **focus group**. Conducting research with a focus group allows you to gather more detailed information and to have more control over the situation and to direct the questions and feedback so that you have the information you need.

Tips for using focus groups for research

- Decide how you want your focus group to be made up. Do you want a group of random people or are you going to be more selective? For example, if you are intending to create a fashion magazine for young men, it may be more useful to research the opinions of the specific target audience of the magazine rather than a random group.

- Make sure that your group are cohesive and will gel well together so that you are sure that everyone will have a chance to give their ideas and opinions.

- Have a plan. This may be a list of questions you want to cover or discussion topics you want the group to cover. Letting the group discuss freely may not be a good idea.

- It may be helpful to have some stimulus material for the group to look at. For example, you could have some front pages of existing fashion magazines for them to look at and comment on.

- Consider how you are going to keep a record of what is said. It may be difficult to make notes and steer the discussion – you could actually record what is said or you could ask a friend to make notes for you. Make sure that they know what you want to find out so that the notes they make are useful. Alternatively, the group members could make notes on a grid you have constructed in advance.

- Finally, you need to analyse your findings and consider how you are going to use the research in your pre-production piece and then incorporate a summary into your report.

Moderator tip

It is important that the focus group research is the right research method for your product as it is time consuming. Think carefully about how to demonstrate how you have used your findings in your report. For example, it may be useful to include a quote from one of your focus group members to support a decision you have made about your product or artefact.

MS2

Pre-production and production approaches

Key Terms

Transitions = The way in which one shot moves on to another in the editing process. The usual transitions are: cuts, fades, wipes and dissolves. The transition is usually matched to the pace and genre of the text.

Continuity = This means that one frame of your storyboard links to the next in a sequence in order to convey the narrative effectively.

Moderator tip

Try to ensure that you include as much information as you can in your storyboard. Avoid just simply describing the shot.

Once your research has been completed you will be ready to embark upon creating your pre-production artefact. If you have done your research well, you will have a more detailed and developed knowledge and understanding of the text you are about to create. For example, if you are creating a script or a storyboard for the opening sequence of a television crime drama then you should now have a good understanding of the codes and conventions of this genre and have a range of options that you can use in your work.

Creating a storyboard

A storyboard is an essential planning device undertaken by most film and television directors. It allows them to think in advance about how they want the narrative to develop and the technical and audio codes they will use to convey this to the audience. Although the storyboard is a print process, you must not view it as such – instead think about it as a way of recording a moving image. You must have thought through and seen the finished moving image in your head before you commit it to paper. This will help you to think about camera shots, angles and **transitions**.

Do not worry that you cannot draw, just ensure that if you say the shot is a close-up, for example, then the visual looks like a close-up. Alternatively, you can take photographs or use a combination of both.

Make sure that you include a range of different shots and transitions in order to hold the attention of your audience. It is also important that there is a sense of **continuity** and that the audience will be able to follow the narrative. Consider the narrative techniques that apply to your chosen genre. For example, crime dramas often employ non-linear narratives in the opening sequence whereby they show the crime committed and then move back in time to the events leading up to the crime. It is also important to consider how you will introduce the characters. Remember the job of the technical codes and editing is to 'show' the audience the characters and narrative and maybe to introduce some enigmas!

A well-constructed and planned storyboard will save you a lot of time when it comes to filming. It is a mistake to rush into filming your sequence without first planning what you want the finished product to look like and the effect you want to have on your audience. When producing a storyboard for your pre-production work, the expectation is that you will produce approximately 20 frames containing the information suggested in this template below:

Shot length	Visuals	Technical codes	Audio	Comment
Transition Transition				

Visuals – Here, in the boxes, you need to draw or place a photograph as an indication of what you want to film. The quality of your drawing is not important – you are not being marked on your art skills, but it must be clear and understandable. Think about the framing of the shot and what you will include in the mise-en-scene.

Comment – This is not usually included in a professional storyboard, but for the purposes of this task, it allows you to explain your decisions including the purpose of the action in the storyboard cell and to highlight the desired effect upon the audience. It may also allow you to demonstrate your broader understanding of the codes and conventions of your chosen genre.

Transition – This is how you want one shot to move into another. Ensure that you use the correct media terminology: fade, wipe, cut and dissolve.

Key Terms

Shot length = This information suggests how long you want the shot to remain on the screen. This should take into account what actually happens in the shot and the overall pace of the extract. For example, if it is a trailer, the pace may be faster than if it is an opening sequence.

Technical codes = This refers to camera shots, angles and editing. Make sure that the technical code you describe in this column matches the drawing in the 'visuals'. Try to make your shots varied and interesting. You will also need to explain any movement of the camera, for example a zoom to a close-up shot, as this is harder to demonstrate on paper.

Audio = Here you need to clearly indicate any sound you want to include, diegetic or non-diegetic including music, dialogue and sound effects.

Key Points

▶ There is a combination of hand-drawn and found images used in the storyboard.

▶ The mise-en-scene is described clearly and in detail using appropriate media terminology.

▶ The shot duration is appropriate, reflecting the format of the film trailer.

▶ There are a range of shots and angles included in the trailer's opening in order to hook the audience and keep their attention.

▶ The visuals accurately represent the description of the shot.

▶ A range of audio codes are employed and described in some detail. The student is clear about what is diegetic and non-diegetic and there is a clear awareness of the effect they want to achieve.

Moderator tip

This storyboard would have benefitted from some analysis of the decisions made and the effect upon the audience. This could have been included in a 'comment' column. The camera instructions should appear BEFORE the mise-en-scene.

Below is an example of a student's storyboard for a film from the crime genre. The student researched the crime genre in general and then focused on the more specific sub-genre of crime involving gangs. The student analysed films including *American Gangster* and *Green Street*. The student also researched the codes and conventions of film trailers and how they attract audiences.

Trailer Storyboard

Shot	Picture	Mise-en-scene	Camera Instructions	Sound
1	UNIVERSAL		Still image of studio logo.	All sound in this shot Non Diegetic (NDie) Heartbeat thump as shot fades in and another when as it fades out. Voice over 1 part a (V/O 1a) of Lewis starts in a slow troubled tone and stereotypical cockney accent. Music: Beetlebum by Blur begins setting a motivated streetwise tone. It is quiet enough to be underscoring the voice over.
			Duration: 6 secs	Transition: Fade in (F/I) from black, Fade out (F/C) to black.
Shot	Picture	Mise-en-scene	Camera Instructions	Sound
2		Interior Setting (INT) Low (L) Back (B) Lighting from barred window creating silhouette of character (Lewis). Shadow of bars on floor. Old orange prison uniform. Old metal bed with no sheets.	Wide Shot (W/S) of prison cell. Mounted (Mnt)	Still NDie sound V/O 1a of Lewis starts in a slow troubled tone continues getting more and more agitated. Beetlebum continues at the same volume.
			Duration: 5 secs	Transition: Fade in (F/I) from black, Fade out (F/O) to black.
Shot	Picture	Mise-en-scene	Camera Instructions	Sound
3		INT L B lighting now with Fill (F) and Low Key (L K) from the right. Lights up face. Lewis sat on bed with head in hands.	Medium Close up (M C/U) of Lewis in profile. Mnt	Still NDie sound V/O 1a continues. Beetlebum continues at the same volume still underscoring voice over.
			Duration: 5 secs	Transition: F/I from black, F/O to black.

Trailer Storyboard

Shot	Picture	Mise-en-scene	Camera Instructions	Sound
4		INT Gang- Baggy clothing, covered faces beating up shopkeeper in a shop. Shop lit by ambient (A) daylight from shop window. Slow motion	W/S Eye Level (E/L) of shop and gang. Mnt Slow Zoom (S/Zm) towards gang and shopkeeper.	NDie V/O 1a continued. Diegetic [Die] Long, slowed down (half time) shouts of gang. Die Ringing of security bell underneath the voice (F/I and F/O) Die Police Car siren fades in quietly. Beetlebum continues still motivated and underscoring.
			Duration: 4 secs	Transition: F/I from black, Cut to next
Shot	Picture	Mise-en-scene	Camera Instructions	Sound
5		INT Security Camera 1 CCTV (Sepia Effect and Pixelated). Ben robbing till. Date and time in the corner. Ambient daylight from left. Ben wearing blood red Adidas jacket.	High Angle (H/A) 45° Mid Shot (M/S) Point of View (POV) Slightly Stretched, Fish eye lens Mnt	NDie V/O 1a continued. Die Police Car siren volume increases slightly. Beetlebum continues still motivated and underscoring.
			Duration: 5 secs	Transition: Cut to next
Shot	Picture	Mise-en-scene	Camera Instructions	Sound
6		INT Security Camera 2 CCTV Date and time in the corner. Gang run out of shot. Ambient light from front.	H/A 45° W/S of shop POV Slightly Stretched Mnt	NDie V/O 1a continued. By now tone has become more motivated and enthusiastic. Die Siren volume increases even more. Beetlebum continues still motivated and underscoring.
			Duration: 4 secs	Transition: Cut to next

Toby Freeman

Creating a script

Another option for a **pre-production** artefact is a script. If this is your choice, your research is the same as if you were creating a storyboard for a trailer or an opening sequence. You must familiarise yourself with the codes and conventions of your selected genre so that you can replicate some of them in your script. Obviously you will also need to pay particular attention to the dialogue and sound in the examples you analyse. It is very important that you format your script correctly according to the type of text you are creating. For example, the format of a situation comedy is different to that of a television drama. There are a range of different places you can use to help you with this. One of the most useful is the **BBC Writers Room**: www.bbc.co.uk/writersroom.

Tips for writing a script

- Consider the narrative format you intend to use and the codes and conventions of your chosen extract. The narrative conventions of, for example, a regular soap opera will be different from a one-off BBC drama.

- Remember that your aim is to attract and maintain the attention of the audience. Open your story with an exciting plot situation or narrative. If it is a trailer, choose some dramatic scenes to illustrate the programme/film's narrative.

- Ensure that your characters are believable so that the audience will want to know what happens to them and therefore stick with your programme. This does not mean that they have to be in believable situations. The television crime drama *Life On Mars* asked us to believe that the policeman travelled back in time to the 1970s but the character of Sam Tyler was such that it caught the imagination of the audience who empathised with his plight. Consider how you will create your characters through the script dialogue and brief descriptions. You can include a supplementary character profile as part of our pre-production submission which will allow you to develop your character ideas more fully.

- Just like with the storyboard, you need to visualise your script and imagine how it would work when filmed and the lines and actions are carried out by real people. It should not be a paper exercise.

- Consider the structure you will employ. Will it be linear? Will you concentrate on one narrative or introduce a series of **interweaving plot strands**?

- Include recognisable genre conventions to help to attract your audience.

Key Terms

BBC writers room = This is a very useful resource to help with script writing. It allows you to look at scripts that have been written for BBC programmes, for example, *Torchwood, Merlin* and *EastEnders,* as well as those from other genres. It also features writers discussing their ideas and inspirations and allows you to download a template specific to a particular format to help you to write your script: www.bbc.co.uk/writersroom/ scriptsmart/bbctapeddrama.pdf. If you are very pleased with your script then you can submit it to the BBC!

Interweaving plot strands = Some television dramas include three or more narratives in their opening sequences and they move the action between these narratives to keep the audience's attention.

Moderator tip

Revisit the work you did at MS1 on genre and narrative to help you to incorporate the relevant features into your script.

Creating a script: an example

Key Features

① Even though you are only writing the script for the opening sequence of a crime drama, you need to give your programme and this particular episode a title. This may give a clue to the genre. The font style used for the BBC scripts is Courier 12 point.

② Usually scripts for dramas start with a 'fade in' to the action. Each new scene should also be on a new page.

③ Next you set out where the action will take place: INT (inside) EXT (outside) and specifically. Adding a number is helpful if you intend to return the action to this location.

④ Information about the scene action is in bold upper case and double spaced below the heading.

⑤ Character names appear in capitals indented around the middle of the page but not centred. This can be the character's name, their role or both.

⑥ Dialogue appears under the name of the character, indented and in lower case.

⑦ As this is not a shooting script, in the industry you would not include camera shots. However, it is sometimes useful to suggest the camera actions to enhance the visuals.

---

① WHICKHAM AND BOYD

"The First Death"

ACT ONE

FADE IN: ②

INT.#1 PUB – NIGHT ③

[THE PUB IS BUSTLING AND THERE IS LOUD NOISE, ④ LAUGHTER, ETC. A GROUP OF GIRLS IS SITTING IN THE CORNER SINGING 'HAPPY BIRTHDAY' TO ONE PARTICULAR GIRL. ANOTHER GIRL, LAURA, GETS UP AND PUTS ON HER COAT.]

        LAURA ⑤
        Hey, guys, I will have to go
        now or I will miss my bus. It's
        been great to meet up with you
        all again. Enjoy the rest of your
        night Sarah. Happy Birthday!

        SARAH
        Shame you can't stay. Thanks for
        coming. ⑥

Laura walks out of the pub.

EXT.#2 ROAD OUTSIDE PUB – SAME NIGHT

[IT IS RAINING HEAVILY. CARS ARE PASSING QUICKLY WITH HEADLIGHTS GLARING. THE BUS PULLS AWAY FROM THE STOP JUST AS LAURA GETS THERE.]

        LAURA
        Damn!

[LAURA LOOKS AT HER WATCH THEN TAKES HER PHONE OUT OF HER POCKET. CU OF PHONE SHOWS IT IS OUT OF ⑦ BATTERY. SHE LOOKS AROUND. THERE IS NO-ONE ABOUT. THE RAIN CONTINUES. HEADLIGHTS APPROACH AND A CAR STOPS AT THE BUS STOP, THE WINDOW WINDS DOWN. THE DRIVER IS NOT VISIBLE. LAURA GETS INTO THE CAR.]

⑧ <u>ACT TWO</u>

EXT. WOODS CLOSE TO PUB. NEXT DAY, EARLY MORNING

**[DETECTIVE INSPECTOR WHICKHAM AND HER SERGEANT BOYD
ARE LOOKING AT A CRIME SCENE. WHICKHAM IS ⑨
A 40 YEAR OLD, TOUGH POLICE OFFICER WHO HAS WORKED
HARD TO GET WHERE SHE IS. SHE IS FORTHRIGHT AND
SPEAKS WITH A STRONG NORTHERN ACCENT. BOYD IS A WELL-
SPOKEN GRADUATE ENTRY YOUNG POLICEMAN WHO KNOWS HIS
STUFF BUT IS NEW TO THIS PATCH. THERE ARE UNIFORMED
POLICE SEARCHING THE IMMEDIATE AREA, CRIME SCENE TAPE
AND TWO POLICE CARS. IT IS STILL RAINING.]**

              D.I. WHICKHAM
      ⑩ (into phone)
We need forensics over here as
soon as possible before the rain
washes all the evidence away!
      (hangs up)   ⑪
What have we got?

              BOYD
Young girl about 20. Dressed for
a night out, looks like. A lot of ⑫
blood but can't say cause of death
until the doc gets here. Looks like
she was dragged here from the road.

FLASHBACK: EXT. MAIN ROAD BY WOODS. PREVIOUS ⑬
EVENING. BLACK AND WHITE

**[A CAR STOPS AND LAURA IS SEEN JUMPING OUT. SHE
STUMBLES AND FALLS. A MAN GETS OUT OF THE DRIVER'S
SIDE AND RUNS AFTER HER. A SCREAM IS HEARD.]**

EXT. WOODS. EARLY MORNING

**[BOYD AND WHICKHAM ARE LEANING OVER THE BODY. ONLY
THE SHOES ARE VISIBLE AND THEY ARE RECOGNISABLE AS
THOSE OF LAURA.]**

          POLICE OFFICER (O.S.)   ⑭
Over here, ma'am. Looks like we've
got something.

Key Features

⑧ Divide your script into acts to suggest changes in the narrative. Here, the location has changed and new characters have been introduced.

⑨ The new characters are briefly described along with the action. This gives a clear indication of the genre through inclusion of iconography. Character profiles can be developed separately.

⑩ Indications of character's actions are placed in parentheses underneath the character's name.

⑪ Remember to indicate when the phone conversation ends.

⑫ The dialogue here reflects understanding of genre codes and conventions.

⑬ You can make your narrative more interesting by including a movement in time like a flashback. The use of black and white indicates to the audience that the narrative has changed.

⑭ O.S. indicates that the character is present but 'out of shot'.

Key Terms

Mock up = This is the term used to describe the planning ideas that a professional designer may engage in before the final product is created. They need to be as close to the finished product as possible so that clients can see what this will look like.

Recce = In a media context this is a pre-filming visit to a location to work out its suitability for photographing or filming. This may take into consideration sound issues and lighting.

Creating a print artefact

There are several options for print artefacts at pre-production and production. These include: DVD covers, magazine pages and film posters. Pre-production work will be a digitally produced **mock up**, and production work will demonstrate a significant development of your ideas. However, as stated earlier, even when producing a mock up, it is important that the finished piece is of a high standard, demonstrating technical and creative proficiency.

Tips for creating successful print work

- Be clear about the codes and conventions of your chosen format. For example, if you choose to create a film poster, it is important that you employ the relevant features to ensure that your work looks as professional as you can make it.

- Use your own images. You do not need to have a high specification camera, many mobile phones can take adequate photographs for the purpose. You cannot be given credit for photographs you have not taken, even if you have manipulated them digitally. Similarly, you should not appear in the photograph yourself as you have then obviously not taken it!

- Give some thought to what you want your photographs/images to look like before you take them. Do a **recce** of possible locations, select appropriate subjects and consider the framing of your photograph.

- If you take a good quality photograph to start with, you will have less editing to do afterwards.

- Consider carefully the style of your piece. Your research, if done well, will have given you ideas for how your print piece should look. Think about the font styles you will use, the layout and design that reflects the genre and the use of colour. Some print styles are more difficult than they seem to replicate; for example, collage-based gossip magazines, so think carefully about your choice of format.

- Don't forget the small details that will make your text look professional, for example the bar codes, parental advisory stamp and the other industry information contained on CD and DVD covers.

- If you are producing magazine pages, for example, make sure that there is a sense of the house style of the publication. Each page must link together stylistically in some way so that it is clear that they are from the same magazine.

- Consider the genre of your print production and ensure that this is reflected in the design choices you make. If you are producing a CD cover for a heavy metal band then the font styles, colour and central images should illustrate the conventions of this genre.

Creating print artefacts: examples

This student researched 'Teen Dramas' and studied the codes and conventions of programmes like *Skins* and films including *Adulthood* looking specifically at characters and narrative. They also researched the codes and conventions of DVD covers and film posters. They then produced a DVD cover for their pre-production artefact and a series of three film posters for their production work. The DVD cover and one of the film posters are reproduced below.

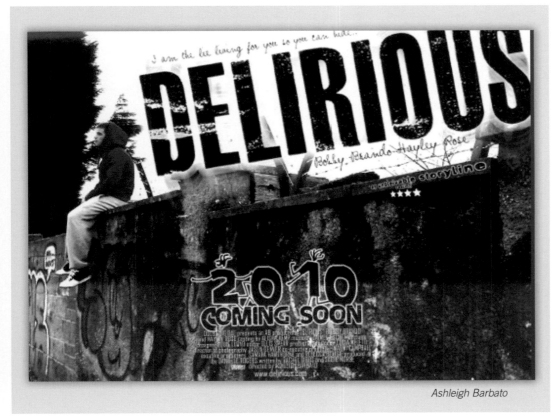

Ashleigh Barbato

Key Points

▶ There is clear evidence in these texts of the research undertaken into the genre conventions. This is evident in the design and layout, choice and use of images and locations.

▶ The DVD cover demonstrates technical ability and creativity. The layout and design is conventional – the thumbnail images and their construction, the blurb, industry information, film title and central image.

▶ The photographs taken are original and there is evidence that thought has gone into the framing. The subject has been well instructed in terms of gesture, expression and clothing. The iconography reflects the 'teen drama' genre.

▶ In the film poster, one of the images from the DVD cover has been re-used which should have been avoided but the poster is very effective in demonstrating the chosen genre. The creative touches, for example the 2010 font style and the layout and design, are sophisticated in their execution. The student has made good use of locations and the subject to suggest the genre.

Key Terms

Post-production = You can add effects to your film after you have finished filming and while you are editing. You can record sounds and add them to you film or add a sound track. You can dub dialogue post-production but this is more complex.

The zoom = Use this camera movement sparingly. Usually as an audience we do not notice the use of the zoom in, for example, a television drama. It should be slow and subtle if it is to be effective.

Moderator tip

Remember to leave plenty of time for editing as this can be the most time-consuming part of the exercise.

Production approaches: Creating a moving image artefact

This will usually develop from a script or storyboard created for pre-production. t is an ambitious choice that demands that you are organised and can meet production deadlines. This is also one of the tasks that you can complete as part of a group. If this is the case, you will need to spend some time discussing which pre-production script/storyboard you intend to develop into production.

Tips for filming and editing

- Check the equipment at your disposal. Make sure that you know how to use it if it is new to you. You may also need to check that it is compatible with your editing software otherwise this will cause problems later.

- Sort out sound. It is invariably the case that students do not give adequate attention to sound, yet there is nothing that can reduce the effectiveness of your film more than poor quality sound. If you are filming outside, you will need to use a suitable microphone for this situation, particularly if you want to pick up dialogue. It is often better to add sound **post-production**.

- Be organised – create a filming schedule and try to stick to it. If you are using actors, it will help that you choose other students who are reliable and can fit in with your requirements. There is nothing worse that casting a lead character who is always late or who doesn't turn up when you need them.

- Use your storyboard – that is what it is for! This will give a structure to your filming. However, it is also a working document and can be tweaked and amended should new ideas appear.

- Just as for a still photo shoot, you need to 'recce' the locations you want to use before you start filming. Check the logistics – for example, if you want to film in school in the evening, do you need to ask permission? If you want to film around school, it is also important to get the permission of people you film, particularly if they are younger members of the school – this may involve contacting parents. You also usually need permission to film in certain locations, for example inside shopping centres.

- Concentrate when you are filming. Always film more footage than you need and for longer – this gives you flexibility when editing. Avoid **zooming** in and out or panning quickly unless you want to create that effect. Be clear about what you want your actors to do and they should know exactly when filming starts and stops.

- Watch the continuity. If you break in filming a scene and then return to film the next day, make sure your actors are dressed the same, the weather hasn't changed dramatically and the locations are similar. This will avoid confusing your audience!

Creating a moving image artefact: example

The screen shots below are from an opening sequence of a gangster heist film made by a student whose pre-production artefact was a storyboard. His research covered examples of this film genre including *Goodfellas*. The actors were other students in the Media Studies group and the location was a domestic kitchen and bathroom. The strength of this piece is that it is not over ambitious and it conveys the narrative through technical and audio codes.

Joe Lunec

Key Points

▶ There is no dialogue in this opening sequence but attention has been paid to sound. This was added post-production and included mood music and heightened sound effects, for example the drumming of fingers on the table and the clicking of the chips.

▶ The use of close-ups and extreme close-ups helps to focus the action, contain it within a limited space and build tension.

▶ Consider how well the shots have been framed, filmed and edited together. This holds the attention of the audience and allows them to accept and become involved in the action.

▶ Attention has been also paid to the lighting which is low key and thus reflects the genre.

MS2

Report writing

Key Terms

A suitably edited blog = Remember that although the language and style of a blog tends to be informal and chatty, you still need to cover all the points listed on this page in order to demonstrate your knowledge. Your writing must be structured and coherent, even when using this format.

Moderator tip

Make sure that you structure your report well, write coherently and demonstrate your knowledge and understanding. Use relevant analytical and media terminology.

㉛ What five key points did you find from your research that helped you to create your artefacts?

Tips for writing a good report

The report must be 1200–1600 words and can be submitted in a range of different formats including: an illustrated report; an essay or a **suitably edited blog**. The first part of the report outlines the research findings that informed your pre-production work and the second part of the report evaluates your production work.

- The report is worth 40 marks, so it is important that you spend some time ensuring that what you write will pick up marks.

- You must stay within the word limit and you should draft and redraft your report in order to achieve this.

- Use the notes you made when completing your pre-production artefact to help you to write the first part of the report.

- Set out your aims clearly at the beginning of your report. This will ensure that your teacher and the moderator are clear about what you set out to do.

'My task was to create a storyboard, a DVD cover and two film posters for a gangster film. In order to accomplish this I had to engage in research of the gangster genre and the specific sub-genre of the gangster heist film.'

Later in the report you can develop how you achieved your aims:

- Briefly discuss the research undertaken and how it informed the pre-production. Include **specific examples** to back up your findings. For example, include references to specific films and state what you discovered when you analysed them that informed your pre-production. Avoid statements like: 'I looked at a lot of front covers of magazines...' without detailing your findings. Your aim is to demonstrate that your research enabled you to discover the key codes and conventions of your chosen genre which you then replicated in your own work.

- Briefly discuss the intended audience for the pre-production and the production and explain how they have been targeted. Remember to justify your decisions.

- Evaluate the strengths and weaknesses of the production through, for example, a comparison of your production with existing media products. Here you can include visuals, for example screen shots from your production, and compare them to shots in a similar existing text.

- If you worked in a group, you will need to evaluate your own contribution, perhaps by comparing your own role to a similar role within a comparable media product. For example, if you were responsible for editing, you may compare your own editing with that in a previously researched text.

- You will need to complete a cover sheet (see example on page 91) outlining your pre-production and production. This will include reference to your contribution to group work where appropriate. You will also need to briefly outline the focus of your report.

Example of a front cover sheet

To be completed by the candidate
Pre-production
For my pre-production I produced a script for the opening sequence of a new British TV crime drama called Wickham and Boyd. I followed the script layout for a BBC programme and tried to keep to the genre conventions of crime by introducing the victim in one scene and then introducing the detectives in the next scene.
Production (including details of your contribution to group work, where relevant)
I worked in a group of 3 to produce the opening sequence of a new crime drama (2 minutes 47 seconds). We had all produced scripts and decided to use Peter's to base our programme on. It was a similar idea to mine. My main responsibility was the editing, although I helped Peter and Mary with the filming as well. For editing I used mac imovie which was quite straightforward, although the sound quality was not as good as we wanted it to be – we did not use an external mic because we didn't have one. It took a lot longer than I thought it would and Peter and Mary often sat and helped me but the final decisions were mine. I also did the titles at the end of the opening sequence. We had some lessons in class on how to use the cameras and imovie but we did not have any help from a technician.
Report
In class we began by talking about the crime dramas on TV at the moment. Our teacher showed us an opening sequence of Death in Paradise and we analysed it as a class. Then we had to look at a minimum of three ourselves. I chose Law and Order UK, CSI New York and Sherlock. My main findings were about typical characters, genre codes and conventions and how the narrative of crime dramas works. For example, they all have similar characters, feature a murder early on in the programme, have lots of enigmas, are set in cities and generally the detectives solve the crime at the end of the episode. I also researched script layouts through the BBC writers room to find out how to construct my script and I studied schedules to see when to put my programme on TV.

NOTICE TO CANDIDATE
The work you submit for assessment must be your own.

If you copy from someone else, allow another candidate to copy from you, or if you cheat in any other way, including plagiarising material, you may be disqualified from at least the subject concerned.

Declaration by Candidate

I have read and understood the **Notice to Candidate** (above). I have produced the attached work without assistance other than that which my teacher has explained is acceptable within the specification.

Signature   Date

This form *must* be completed by all candidates and *must* accompany work submitted for moderation.

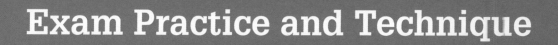

Exam Practice and Technique

Key Terms

Toolkit for Analysis = This is essentially a list of key words or phrases that you know you need to use when, for example, analysing a particular text or responding to a bullet point in the examination. For example, if the bullet point asks you to comment on 'visual codes', you will know what you need to include in your answer.

Aide-memoire = A device or prompt to enable you to remember certain things. The grids here are 'aide-memoires' for aspects of the media specification. Some people also find a mnemonic useful.

Using a 'Toolkit for Analysis'

In this subject you are required to study how a range of media texts are constructed and the meanings contained within them, before you can discuss how audiences and users respond to them. You must be prepared to transfer your knowledge so that you are equipped and ready to analyse any unseen text in the examination. The key is to build up a **Toolkit for Analysis**. In preparation you need to analyse a range of different texts – there is an expectation at this level that you can discuss the texts in an articulate manner employing relevant analytical and technical vocabulary. The Media Studies examination does not test memory or remembered facts; it tests your ability to demonstrate your knowledge and understanding of those texts, their effect upon audiences and their purpose.

The grids below work as a check list or **aide-memoire** so that when you see the stimulus material and the bullet points in the MS1 examination, you know what points you need to include in your response. Some are relevant to both print and moving image and some are more specific.

TECHNICAL AND AUDIO CODES	VISUAL CODES/IMPACT
✓ Camera shots	✓ Use of colour
✓ Camera angles	✓ Iconography
✓ Camera movement	✓ Gesture
✓ Lighting	✓ Expression
✓ Editing – pace, special effects	✓ Mise-en-scene
✓ Graphics	✓ Use of graphics
Sound – diegetic and non-diegetic	✓ Images
✓ Sound effects	✓ The look
✓ Music	✓ Lighting
✓ Dialogue	
✓ Voice-overs	

LAYOUT AND DESIGN	LANGUAGE AND MODE OF ADDRESS
✓ Selection and use of images	✓ Lexis
✓ Graphics	✓ Tone
✓ Colour	✓ Use of vocabulary
✓ Structure of text	✓ Hyperbole
✓ Font styles	✓ Quotations

NARRATIVE CODES	CHARACTERS
✓ Narrative strands	✓ Representation issues
✓ Construction – linear/circular	✓ Relevance
✓ Generic conventions	✓ Place in narrative
✓ Enigmas	✓ Relationships
✓ Character relevance/purpose	✓ Theory – Propp
✓ Action codes	✓ Visual codes linked to character – clothing, gesture, expression
✓ Filming techniques	
✓ Manipulation of time and space	
✓ Theory – Todorov	

Examiner tip
When you are viewing audio visual texts or analysing print texts in class, experiment in using grids or other formats to help you when making notes.

32 What different types of audio codes may you hear in a text? For example, dialogue.

Taking notes

Note-taking is a skill that needs to be practised before it is perfected. In the MS1 examination, if the stimulus is audio-visual, you will be guided to making notes during and between viewings two and three. This is then the last time that you will see the material, so it is vitally important that when you look back on your notes, they can help you to answer the questions. If the stimulus material is print based, you still need to spend some time considering your responses to the questions and making notes about the texts you have been given to analyse.

Tips

- Read the questions that refer to the stimulus material carefully at the beginning. This will be Q1 and the first part(s) of Q2.

- Use the bullet points given for Q1 to guide your note-taking. You must respond to each bullet point in your response to this question.

- Consider how you will make notes that will be useful in answering the question. Grids are very useful for this task, they avoid you writing too much and if they are well designed, they will help you to focus on what you need and to select what is appropriate.

- Avoid merely writing down a description of what you see on the screen. Some students fall into this trap when the stimulus material has an obvious narrative, for example the opening sequence of the film. Copious notes about what happened or a chronological account of the events will not help you to answer the question. You will remember what happened as you will see it three times, what you will not remember is how the camera showed you what happened through, for example, shots, angles and editing, or how the sound added to the narrative.

- If one of the bullet points is, for example, technical codes, you cannot write down all the examples you see in the extract. Be selective. Choose a range of shots and write them down on your grid.

- Always consider the purpose and effect of the technical code; never just name the shot and then move on, or list shots without analysing their use. The technical codes grid on page106 suggests that you look for examples during the first and second viewing and then develop this by looking at purpose and effect in the final viewing.

- Listen carefully to the audio in an audio-visual text. Students, in their responses, are generally weaker when discussing audio and do not analyse it in detail. Make notes in your grid on the different types of audio used in the text, its purpose and the possible effect upon the audience.

- This is the same for the print texts used as stimulus. Make notes on the purpose and effect of the layout and design, if this is required, not forgetting to analyse why those decisions have been made.

Opening paragraphs

As was stated earlier in this study guide, it is important that all your responses to examination questions are structured and coherent. It is important that you demonstrate your broad knowledge and understanding to the examiner. Having a clear introduction, main body and conclusion to your response will help you to achieve a more sophisticated answer. This is particularly true with regard to Questions 2c and 3, which are the more challenging MS1 questions. Your opening paragraph to these questions is very important. It should:

- Define any key terminology showing that you understand the meaning. It may be useful to demonstrate your understanding of a key word in an audience-focussed question; for example, audience positioning. If you do this in your opening paragraph, you show your understanding of the term and provide a focus for the rest of your response.

- Demonstrate your broad understanding of the concept, for example representation. Do not launch into an analysis of your three chosen texts straightaway, place them into a context.

- Include key terminology in your opening paragraph that you can then apply to the analysis of your texts. For a question on representation you may want to include terms like construction, ideology and mediation.

Example question

Explore how media texts target different audiences.

Opening paragraph example:

The aim of all media texts, both print and audio visual, is to target an audience who will then be consumers of the product. In a competitive media-saturated society it is vital that strategies are used in order to target the appropriate audience. Some texts will target a specific, niche audience and the aim of other texts will be to appeal to as wide an audience as possible. All texts are in competition with other existing products and therefore it is essential that their strategies work. The text may also be targeting a primary, secondary and in some cases a tertiary audience.

I have chosen three different texts to demonstrate how they use different strategies to target their audience...

Examiner tip

Do not start to analyse your examples until you have shown that you understand what the question is asking.

quickfire

(33) What key points would you make in a question where the focus was on how different audiences respond to the same media text?

MS1 Checklist

Question 1: Textual analysis

Can I?

- Use the correct media terminology to analyse a range of different texts?
- Use a range of analytical terminology to analyse a range of media texts?
- Analyse technical codes, their purpose and effect?
- Analyse audio codes, their purpose and effect?
- Analyse visual codes, their purpose and effect?
- Analyse narrative devices in media texts?
- Demonstrate understanding of the genre conventions of different media texts?
- Analyse the effect of layout and design in print texts?
- Analyse language and mode of address in different media texts, both print and audio visual?

Representation questions

Can I?

- Write an opening paragraph related to a range of representation questions?
- Use the relevant terminology when discussing representation?
- Use relevant examples to show understanding of the ways in which:
  - age
  - gender
  - ethnicity
  - issues
  - events
  - regional and national identity

  are represented in the media today?

Audience questions

Can I?

- Write an opening paragraph related to a range of audience questions?
- Use a range of specific examples to support points about audience?
- Explore, with examples, how audiences may respond differently to the same media text?
- Explore, with examples, how texts construct audiences?
- Explore, with examples, how texts position audiences?
- Explore, with examples, how texts target and appeal to audiences?
- Explore, with examples, the ways in which audiences can be categorised?

MS1 question 3 response 30 marks

Using your own detailed examples explore the representations of women in the media today.

This is an extract, not a complete response to MS1, question 3. The commentary indicates how the response could have been improved.

Tom's answer

① Representation in the media is the way in which media texts like magazines and television programmes offer the audience versions of reality and present certain social groups in a particular way. All representations are constructions, media texts are not 'windows on the world'. The way in which the representation is constructed is influenced by the messages and ideas ② that the producers of the text want to convey. It is also linked to the expectations of the target audience. ③

Different representations have a different purpose according to the genre of the text, the context and the target audience. For example, with regard to representations of gender, women are represented in different ways in the media today depending on the specific text and its context. It is a simple statement to say that all representations of women are negative, it is more complex than that. ④

On the front cover of February's issue of *Cosmopolitan* the representation is constructed to offer the ideology that women are defined by their body image and their lifestyle. Pixie Lott ⑤ engages in a direct mode of address with the reader and in her body language and expression she appeals to both male and female audience. The cover lines suggest the discourse ⑥ of a sexual relationship, fashion and female narcissism.

In the trailer for *Salt*, ⑦ the representation is of a woman as an action hero. The technical codes and editing of the film trailer construct the representation of Agent Salt performing what are seen to be usually masculine tasks, for example being chased, shot at and jumping from a bridge onto a moving wagon. However, her representation is ambiguous as she is very glamourised and played by Angelina Jolie who tends to depict this dual gender appeal role.

Examiner commentary

① This candidate includes an introduction which anchors their understanding of the question and demonstrates their broad knowledge of the concept. They avoid jumping straight into an analysis of their examples; instead their introduction serves to place their examples within a context.

② Here they could have used the media term 'ideology' to make the response more sophisticated and to demonstrate media knowledge.

③ This comment incorporates the three key areas of the text, the representation contained within it and the audience who will consume it.

④ Here the candidate makes a sophisticated point that representations differ according to the context thus demonstrating a broader knowledge of the concept. The expectation is that this will be later backed up by a specific example.

⑤ The example used here is specific and not general, this allows the candidate to explore the text in more detail, backing up points made.

⑥ The candidate uses media vocabulary specific to the text analysed.

⑦ The second example used is from a different media form and illustrates a different type of representation of women. The response develops to consider specifically how the representation is constructed. It may have helped to discuss the shots in more detail maybe to illustrate the 'male gaze' in order to back up the point that the representation is constructed to appeal to men and women.

The candidate should develop these examples further and include a third from another media form.

Summative comments

This response is competent and is on the way to a good mark/level. The candidate has included an opening paragraph that employs relevant vocabulary and demonstrates that they have an overview of the concept. They show their awareness that representations are constructions and are used for a purpose. They can also discuss how the representation changes according to its context and are aware that representations are complex. They also are able to develop their initial general points by analysing specific media texts from a range of formats in detail using media terminology.

MS1 question 2c response 16 marks

Using your own detailed examples explore the representations of age in the media today.

This is an extract, not a complete response to MS1, question 2c. The commentary indicates how the response could have been improved.

Tom's answer

① There are lots of images of age in the media today. The representation of young people in the media today is mainly negative. There are very few positive representations. There are positive and negative representations of old people.

② In newspapers and on television news programmes the representation of young people is mainly negative. They are seen to be involved in crime, to cause trouble and are given names like 'hoodies'. ③ In the recent student demonstrations over tuition fees the media represented them as violent. I think that this is a bad representation, young people are not all like that....

④ Examples of texts showing representations of young people are *The Inbetweeners* and *Kidulthood*. ⑤ In *The Inbetweeners* the representation of young teenage boys is negative. The programme only shows them concerned about drinking and sex. In Kidulthood the young people are shown to be violent, the representation is negative, they swear, fight and take drugs...

⑥ Old people like to read Saga magazine. It is aimed at people 50 and above. There is an image of Michael Caine on the front cover and the audience will be able to relate to him. ⑦ He plays a similar role of an older, angry man in Harry Brown. ⑧ The colours used on Saga magazine are warm and gentle as older people don't like bright colours. The writing is big and spaced out as older people have trouble seeing small print...

Examiner commentary

① This is a very general opening paragraph. The candidate does not define what they understand by 'age' nor do they demonstrate an overview of their understanding of the concept of representation in a media context. (see earlier for guidance on writing opening paragraphs)

② The candidate then continues to be very general in their response – they refer to 'newspapers' and television news' but they must analyse specific examples, e.g. *BBC News at 10* on a specific evening or a particular issue of the *Daily Mail*.

③ The example of the student riots is a good one but the candidate has not anchored it in a specific media text. They are also beginning to produce an opinion-led response that does not demonstrate media knowledge and the ability to explore and analyse media texts.

④ These are good examples – the expectation is that 2/3 examples from more than one media format will be used in this response.

⑤ However, the points made are simple and anchor on the discussion of positive and negative. There is no awareness of the context and purpose of the representation and its effect upon an audience: *The Inbetweeners* is a situation comedy and the aim is to use recognisable stereotypes to make the audience laugh. *Kidulthood* is a hard hitting social realist film whose purpose is to shock.

⑥ Although the comments regarding *Saga* magazine are relevant – this is the stimulus material for Q1 and therefore must not be used to answer this question.

⑦ *Harry Brown* is a good example and could have been developed here.

⑧ Here the candidate makes worryingly simple comments and reinforces simple stereotypes of older people. The expectation for a higher mark is that the response will explore the representations in a more sophisticated way and consider how they are constructed by the producers of the text.

Summative comments

This response is less secure and the extracts from it are more indicative of a 9–10 mark response. It is clear that this candidate's understanding is emerging but undeveloped. They do include an opening paragraph and do not make the mistake of jumping straight into their textual examples. However, this is more assertive without evidence; it does not really show their understanding of the concept. They make the mistake of using the examination stimulus material as an example; this has affected their final mark. Their other examples are appropriate but the analysis is simple and there is no awareness of the context and purpose of the representation.

Q&A

MS1 question 3 response 30 marks

Using your own detailed examples explore the ways in which media texts target audiences.

This is an extract, not a complete response to MS1, question 3. The commentary indicates how the response could have been improved.

Tom's answer

① All media texts need to target an audience to ensure that their product sells in a competitive market. This means that they are aware of their audience and they include features in the text that will encourage them to consume the product. Different media texts will use different strategies to appeal to audiences. The aim of some texts is to target a niche audience, other texts want a broader appeal to maximise the audience. ② The way in which the text is constructed will help to target a specific audience. In magazines the choice of the front page image, the cover and sell lines, the layout and design and the language and mode of address all work together in order to target the specific audience of the magazine. For example, in Cosmopolitan magazine … ③

④ A trailer for a film uses a range of strategies to attract audiences. There will be clues in the trailer to suggest the genre of the film to attract fans of that genre. For example, in the trailer for *Salt*, the shots chosen clearly show that this is an action film. Agent Salt is shown by the camera shots and editing, in a chase sequence and a shoot out. Angelina Jolie is also billed clearly, which would target fans of the star. The audio codes include a voice-over, snippets of dialogue and dramatic music, which will again target audiences who want to be excited and thrilled and who may want to escape from everyday life. ⑤

⑥ A media text can also target an audience through positioning. This is often the case in film or television texts. In a scene from the recent series of *CSI: Miami* the camera placed the audience at the scene of a crime that was about to happen. The audience were positioned to be part of the action by the use of a hand-held camera and rapid editing. This made the audience feel part of the action and targeted those who like to watch crime dramas.

Examiner commentary

① This candidate includes an introduction that defines the key word 'target' in the question and presents an overview including why audiences need to be targeted, showing their broader understanding. They also use relevant terms, for example 'niche audience'.

② The candidate here demonstrates that they can use relevant media terminology to analyse the text. By using the word 'constructed' they show a more sophisticated understanding of the concept.

③ The candidate now needs to apply their understanding of how the text is constructed in order to target an audience by analysing a specific magazine in detail. They must avoid a general response that only refers to 'magazines'.

④ This is a good example to use to discuss targeting through genre. The candidate could have developed their analysis of specific shots in more detail.

⑤ They also begin to implicitly cite some relevant theories; for example, uses and gratifications, which could have been further developed to suggest how targeting can elicit a response from an audience.

⑥ Here, the candidate develops their answer further by using a third, different example and by introducing an additional point with regard to audience targeting through positioning. This avoids them making the same points about each example and demonstrates their understanding of the relationship between text and audience.

Summative comments

This is a potentially strong response which could access the higher mark bands (21+). The candidate has effectively focussed on the key word from the question and demonstrates their understanding of audience in this opening paragraph. They use media vocabulary relevant to the text to be analysed, for example magazines. Although we do not have their analysis of *Cosmopolitan*, the expectation is that they will have applied their introductory comments specifically to this text. They effectively refer to a different strategies used to target audiences and therefore avoid making the same points twice. They use relevant textual examples to analyse technical codes and positioning and they refer to specific examples from their chosen texts.

Glossary of technical terms

It is very important in all your MS1 responses and your MS2 report that you employ relevant technical and analytical vocabulary. Doing so will demonstrate your understanding and allow you to produce a more articulate and informed response. The following list is not exhaustive but includes useful media terminology to help you to develop a more sophisticated analysis of texts.

ACCENT – the way in which the inhabitants of a particular region speak. For, example, the Scouse accent belongs to those who live or originate from Liverpool.

ACTION CODE – something that happens in the narrative that tells the audience that some action will follow, for example in a scene from a soap opera, a couple are intimate in a bedroom and the camera shows the audience the husband's car pulling up at the front of the house.

ACTIVE AUDIENCE – this describes an audience who responds to and interprets the media texts in different ways and who actively engages with the messages in the ways suggested here.

ANCHORAGE – the words that accompany an image (still or moving) give the meaning associated with that image. If the caption or voice-over are changed then so is the way in which the audience interprets the image. An image with an anchor is a closed text; the audience are given a preferred reading. An image without an anchor is an open text as the audience can interpret it as they wish. The same image of a local school in a local newspaper could run a negative or a positive headline, which would change the way in which the same image is viewed by the reader.

APPEAL – adverts try to appeal to something within us so that we will buy into the product. They may appeal to our greed or our need for security. Many adverts use the 'herd instinct' appeal by persuading us that everyone else has the product and we will be left behind. Sex appeal is used to sell everything from beauty products to cheese!

BRAND – that which identifies one company's products from those of another. The branding may be clearly identifiable by a name, logo or some other trademark, for example the font style used by Kellogg's or the Nike swoosh!

BRAND IDENTITY – the associations the audience makes with brand. This is built up over time. The brand **Nike** suggests good quality sports clothing that is also fashionable as leisure wear. The high-budget advertising campaigns and sponsorship at world events have helped to reinforce this brand image over time.

CAMPAIGN – run by an advertising agency, this incorporates all the ways in which the product is promoted, for example packaging, radio, TV, Internet and print adverts.

CANNED LAUGHTER – pre-recorded laughter that is added to a television or radio programme post-production. It serves to prompt the audience and encourage them to laugh at the funny bits of the programme.

CAPTION – words that accompany an image that explain its meaning.

CHIAROSCURO LIGHTING – low-key lighting used to create areas of light and darkness, particularly in black and white films. The effect is to suggest unease and tension within the scene.

CIRCULAR NARRATIVE – this is where the narrative starts at the end and then explores the action up to that point. It is sometimes only at the very end of the film or television programme that the narrative makes sense.

CLIFFHANGER – a narrative device used at the end of an episode of a drama where the narrative is left unresolved. This encourages the audience to watch the next episode to find out what happened.

CODES – signs within a media text that give clues to the text's meaning.

COVER LINES – these suggest the content to the reader and often contain teasers and rhetorical questions.

COLLOQUIALISM – an informal expression that is more often used in casual conversation than in formal speech or writing.

CONSUMABLE PRODUCTS – these are the products that we use regularly and that need to be replaced. Some audiences are loyal to a particular brand, whereas others may be persuaded to change as a result of successful marketing devices.

CONNOTATION – the meanings attached to that description, for example the red car in the advert suggests speed and power.

CONSTRUCTION – how a media text is put together. The way in which it is constructed will affect how the audience responds to it. Elements of the construction may include: the caption, the choice of image and the language used.

CONSUME – another way of saying how an audience uses a media text. We are all consumers of different media texts.

CONTEXT – with regard to representation, this means where the representation appears, for example the representation of young people may be different in a news bulletin compared to a situation comedy.

CONTEXTUAL ADVERTISING – a form of targeted advertising where, as a result of the information the user has entered on the site, a related advert will appear.

CONVENTIONS – what the audience expects to see in a particular media text, for example the conventions of science fiction films may include: aliens, scientists, other worlds, gadgets, representations of good and evil, etc. Useful headings to discuss conventions are: characters, setting, iconography, narrative, technical codes and representation.

COPY – the writing on the media text.

CULTURAL COMPETENCE – within a media context, this concept suggests that the cultural competence of an audience is the shared knowledge, related to their cultural understanding of that audience, which means that they will take a particular pleasure from a media text.

DECODING – the different ways in which the audience interprets the messages contained within a media text.

DEMOGRAPHIC PROFILING – dividing consumers into groups based on age, sex, income, education, occupation, household size, marital status, home ownership or other factors. This information can help advertisers determine their target audience for particular products and develop adverts that focus on a specific demographic.

DEMONSTRATIVE ACTION – this is when the audience can see the product being used in the advert, for example the hair dye being applied or the floor being cleaned.

DENOTATION – the description of what you can see/hear in a media text, for example the car in the advert is red.

DESENSITISATION – a psychological process that suggests that audiences who are exposed regularly to acts of violence through films and video games, for example, are increasingly less likely to feel empathy or concern when exposed to violence, bad language or other forms of aggressive behaviour.

DIALECT – the particular words that have their origins in a specific region and are used by the inhabitants of that region and may be unknown to others.

DIEGETIC SOUND – sound that can be seen, for example the sound of a gun firing, the cereal being poured into the bowl in an advert, etc.

DISCOURSE – the topics and language used by a media text. There are certain topics that would never appear as the discourse of a magazine like *Glamour*. The discourse tends to centre on body image and how to look good.

DOMINANT IDEOLOGY – this is the point of view of the creators of the media text. This may be implicit or explicit as is evident in texts like popular newspapers.

DRIVETIME PROGRAMMES – the programmes that are scheduled between 5 and 7 pm and are designed for listeners who are driving home.

EDITING – the way in which the shots are put together to create a particular effect. Editing can be described in terms of pace and the transitions that are employed.

EDITORIAL – the part of the newspaper written, supposedly, by the editor who comments on the day's stories. It offers an opportunity for the paper to express its views and to demonstrate its ideology.

EFFECT – the effect the technical code will have upon the audience. It may make them feel uncomfortable (an extreme close-up), or intrigue them and therefore encourage them to continue watching.

ELLIPSIS – where sentences are incomplete and are finished with a set of dots, the words need to be filled in by the reader.

ENCODING – the ideas and messages that are contained within the media text. These may reflect the ideas of the producers of the text.

ENIGMA CODE – a narrative device which increases tension and audience interest by only releasing bits of information, for example teasers in a film trailer. Narrative strands that are set up at the beginning of a drama/film that makes the audience ask questions. This is part of a restricted narrative.

ETHNOCENTRIC – if a newspaper is ethnocentric then it tends to be concerned with issues that are close to home and will more directly interest the readers. For example, a local newspaper may only run a national or international story if a local person is involved.

EVENT – in media terms, an event is something that occurs or is about to occur and is of interest to an audience. Events come in a range of shapes and forms and can be local, national or international.

EVENT TELEVISION – this term describes programmes like, for example, the final of *Strictly Come Dancing* that attracts a big audience, is highly publicised and therefore becomes an 'event'.

EXPERT WITNESSES – this is where a media text like a film poster includes quotes from experts who the audience will trust, for example *Empire Magazine*. If they give the film positive reviews and we trust them, we are more likely to go and see it.

FEMME FATALE – this was the female character in a film noir. Her main characteristics were that she was beautiful, seductive, amoral and able to manipulate the male protagonist to do her will. She was usually destroyed at the end of the film.

FILM NOIR- this was a style, rather than genre of films from the 1940s and 50s that had common cinematic features including low-key lighting. They were crime dramas involving recognisable character types and settings.

FLY ON THE WALL DOCUMENTARY – a documentary programme filmed using hidden cameras. The suggestion is that the subjects of the film will behave more naturally and as a result reality will be captured.

FORMULAIC STRUCTURE – this is where the text has a clear structure that is recognisable and rarely changes. For example, the front cover of a glamour magazine has key conventions and the audience has expectations of what will appear on which page throughout the publication.

GATEKEEPERS – the people responsible for deciding which stories will appear in the newspaper. They are usually the editor and senior journalists. They will open the gate for some stories and shut it for others.

GENRE – media texts can be grouped into genres that all share similar conventions. Science Fiction is a genre, as are teenage magazines, etc.

GRAPHICS – precise type of design and in media terms means the titles and credits in a film or on television, the seemingly hand-drawn, but usually computer-generated illustrations in a games magazine, for example.

HAND-HELD CAMERA – a style of filming whereby a decision has been made not to use the Steadicam on the camera but to allow the camera to move freely during filming. This gives a jerky style of filming that suggests realism and makes the audience feel involved in the action.

HARD SELL ADVERTISING – 'in your face 'advertising. These adverts are usually short, loud and clearly tell you the price of the product, what it does and where you can get it. The mode of address is direct.

HOOK – the element of a media text that catches the attention of the audience and draws them in. On a film poster it may be the image, the tag line or the copy.

HOUSE STYLE – what makes the magazine recognisable to its readers every issue. The house style is established through the choice of colour, the layout and design, the font style and the general 'look' of the publication.

HYBRID GENRES – are media texts that incorporate features of more than one genre. *Strictly Come Dancing* includes features of reality television, game show and an entertainment programme.

HYPERBOLE – over exaggerated language used to create a dramatic effect.

HYPODERMIC NEEDLE MODEL – a now largely outdated effects theory which suggests that the audience are a mass that behave the same way in response to a media text. The media text injects ideas into the minds of the assumed passive audience who will respond as one. It is most usually used to support the idea that violent media texts, for example video games and films, cause the audience to behave violently.

ICONIC REPRESENTATION – the actual image of the product appears in the advert to show the audience what it looks like, for example the image of the perfume bottle is usually featured in fragrance adverts.

ICONOGRAPHY – the props, costumes, objects and backgrounds associated with a particular genre; for example, in a police series you would expect to see uniforms, blue flashing lights, scene of crime tape and police radios.

IDEOLOGY – the values and messages held by the producers of a media text that may appear in the text itself. In the case of newspapers, it may be clear from the stories chosen in, for example, *The Daily Mail*, what that paper thinks about asylum seekers or the Euro.

IMPERATIVE (THE) – words or phrases that contain a command or order. They usually end with an exclamation mark, for example 'get Your Free Gift Now!'

INTERTEXTUALITY – using one text within another. For example, the use of a fairytale within a music video. Gwen Stefani uses the narrative features of *Rapunzel* in her music video *The Sweet Escape*.

JUMP LINE – this appears at the end of a cover line and usually tells the audience which page to turn to in order to read the full story.

LAYOUT – the way in which a page has been designed to attract the target audience. This includes the font styles used, the positioning of text and images and the use of colour.

LEXIS – the choice of words used. This may be linked to a particular genre, for example the lexis of science fiction can be scientific and technical.

LINEAR NARRATIVE – where the narrative unfolds in chronological order from beginning to end.

LOOK (THE) – used to describe the way in which the image on a print text is looking. For example, the gaze of the model on the front of a glamour magazine may be direct and challenging the audience.

MAGAZINE PROGRAMME – a genre of radio programme that, like a magazine, includes a range of features, for example music, chat, news, gossip and interviews.

MARK OF QUALITY – this is usually the film logo, the director's name or references to other successful films made by this director. These are included to convince the audience that this new film is a quality product.

MASCULINITY – the state of 'being a man' and this can change as society changes. It is essentially what being a man means to a particular generation. This is then reflected in media texts.

MASTHEAD – the name of the magazine and, along with the font style, may give clues to the sub-genre.

MEDIA TEXT – a product of a media industry, for example a film, advertisement, television programme, magazine, etc.

MISE–EN–SCENE – in analysis of moving image – how the combination of images in the frame creates meaning. How individual shots in a film or photograph have been composed.

MODE OF ADDRESS – the way in which a media text 'speaks to' its target audience. For example, teenage magazines have a chatty informal mode of address; the news has a more formal mode of address.

MOTIF – a current thematic element used by an artist and recognised by fans of that artist. It is usually established by the iconography surrounding the artist including props, costumes and settings.

NARRATIVE – the 'story' that is told by the media text. All media texts, not just fictional texts, have a narrative. For example, magazines have a clear beginning, middle and end. Most narratives are linear and follow a specific structure (Todorov).

NATIONAL IDENTITY – the representation of a country as a whole, encompassing its culture, traditions, language, and politics. This includes the characteristics of the country that are clearly definable to other nations.

NEW MAN – a term introduced to describe a new breed of men. These men rejected sexist attitudes; were in touch with their feminine side and were therefore not afraid to be sensitive and caring and could sometimes be seen in a domestic role.

NEWS AGENDA – the list of news stories that may appear in a particular newspaper. Some stories of the day will never appear on the agenda of certain newspapers because they will not interest their readers.

NON-DIEGETIC SOUND – sound that is out of the shot, for example a voice-over, romantic mood music.

NON-LINEAR NARRATIVE – here the narrative manipulates time and space. It may begin in the middle and then include flashbacks and other narrative devices.

OPINION LEADERS – those in positions of power who aim to persuade an audience of their point of view (ideology). Within the media these may be newspaper editors, programme producers or film directors.

PASSIVE AUDIENCE – an audience that does not engage actively with the text. They are more likely to accept the preferred meaning of the text without challenge. This also suggests that passive audiences are more likely to be directly affected by the messages contained within the text.

PLATFORM – a range of different ways of communicating, for example television, newspapers, Internet, etc.

PLUG/PUFF – these appear in all newspapers and usually run across the top of the front page. Their aim is to show what else is in the paper and will usually contrast to the serious news on the front page to broaden the audience appeal.

POLYSEMIC – texts that have more than one meaning contained within them are termed 'polysemic'. They can be interpreted in different ways by an audience.

POP-UPS – a type of Internet advertisement where an advert literally 'pops up' on the screen when the web page is being used. Their aim is to attract web traffic or capture email addresses.

POSITIONING – where the camera, the editing or the audio codes place the audience in a particular position. This may be emotionally to empathise more clearly with a character, or to have expectations of how the narrative will develop.

PRODUCT ENDORSEMENT – the use of celebrities, members of the public, experts, etc., to say how good the product is. If the endorser is admired and believable, the audience may be persuaded to buy the product.

PRODUCTION VALUES – the features of a media text that show how much it has cost to make. A high budget programme or film is recognisable by its settings, use of stars, more complex editing and soundtrack, for example.

PROFILE – with regard to, for example, television channels and radio stations, this means how they would be defined. This may include their target audience, their aims and their ethos.

PROMISES OF PLEASURE – this is what the trailer or film poster tells the audience they will get out of the film. They may laugh, or cry, or be more terrified than ever before!

PROTAGONISTS – the main character(s) that are central to the action.

PURPOSE – the reason why the technique has been used in the media text. It may be to involve the audience, to develop the narrative or to create tension.

REGIONAL IDENTITY – the way in which a particular area of a country is defined by the accent, dialect, dress and customs of its inhabitants.

REGISTER – the spoken or written register of a media text is the range and variety of language used within the text. This will change according to the purpose of the text and its target audience.

REPRESENTATION – the way in which key sections of society are presented by the media. A range of representations will include examples of: gender, ethnicity, age, issues, events and regional and national identity. For example, one important example in the media is how women are represented in magazines.

RHETORICAL QUESTIONS – questions to which an answer is not expected. The use of them in media texts like trailers serves to introduce enigmas in the minds of an audience. They will only find out the answers by watching the whole film and as such they are a marketing tool.

RICH TEXTS – texts that you could use for more than one area of the specification. For example, the trailer and key scenes from *Slumdog Millionaire* can be used to discuss representations of national identity, age, gender and the issue of poverty as well as being a useful text to use when analysing audience responses and targeting.

SELECTION – this is what is chosen by the creators of the text to be included in the text. This selection may reflect the ideology of the text and decisions have been made about what to include and what to leave out.

SELL LINES – the 'extras' over and above the usual content, for example chances to win something.

SIGN/CODE – something which communicates meaning, for example colours, sounds. The meaning of the sign changes according to the context, for example the colour red can mean passion, love, danger or speed, depending on how and where it is used.

SILVER SURFER – an older person who is computer literate and uses the net to purchase goods and find out information.

SLOGAN – a catchy phrase that is memorable and thus becomes associated with the product.

SOFT SELL ADVERTISING – these adverts are much more subtle and attempt to sell a lifestyle rather than just a product. The actual product is not always obvious until the end of the advert.

STAR PERSONA – this term is used to refer to those music stars that have an identity beyond their ability to make music. That persona may be demonstrated through character and personality and be evident in other media texts, for example magazine interviews, advertising campaigns, etc.

STEREOTYPE – an exaggerated representation of someone or something. It is also where a certain group are associated with a certain set of characteristics, for example all Scotsmen are mean, blondes are dumb, etc. However, stereotypes can also be quick ways of communicating information in adverts and dramas, for example the rebellious teenager in a soap opera, as they are easily recognisable to audiences.

STOCK CHARACTERS – easily recognisable characters, often stereotypes that support the main characters.

STORY ARC – the way in which the narrative progresses from the beginning to the end of the text. A story arc may also cross episodes.

STORY SYNOPSIS – the summing up of the storyline to give the user an idea of what happens in the film, television programme or DVD.

STRAPLINES – these are mostly found on tabloids where the headline does not give much information about the story. The strapline gives more information about the main story.

STRIPPING – a scheduling technique used in radio and television whereby the same programme or genre of programme is scheduled at the same time every day.

SUB-GENRE – smaller groups within a larger type of media text. Within the magazine genre the sub-genres may include music, gaming and home-improvement magazines.

SUSPENSION OF DISBELIEF – this is where the audience are involved in the action and do not question impossible aspects of it, for example the sound of violins on a deserted beach in a romantic film.

SYMBOL – a sign which is understood to refer to something other than itself. A woman wearing a red dress in an advertisement may symbolise that she is passionate or dangerous.

TAG LINES – the short slogan-like phrases that sum up a film. They are usually found on film posters and other print promotional material.

TARGET AUDIENCE – the people at whom the media text is aimed.

TEASER CAMPAIGN – this is when the film posters are part of a sequence whose aim is to release more information about the film gradually in the run up to the release. The campaign employs enigmas to catch the interest of the audience by withholding information.

TECHNICAL CODES – these are the way in which the text has been produced to communicate meanings and include:

Camera shots – for example, close-up shots are often used to express emotion.

Camera angles – a shot of a character from above makes them appear more vulnerable.

Editing – the way in which the shots move from one to the other (transitions), for example fade, cut, etc. This may increase the pace and therefore the tension of the text.

Audio – how the sound is used to communicate meaning – voice-over, dialogue, music, SFX, etc.

THUMBNAILS – the small drawings that represent the plot situations from the game. They usually appear on the back of DVD or games covers.

TOKENISM – this is where a media text includes a few members of a minority group, for example some plus size models in a glamour magazine. This appears to redress the balance but in fact, as the group is in the minority they have no real power within the text and their 'difference' from the norm is also highlighted. Tokenism also tends to present a stereotypical view of that group so that audiences can recognise them easily.

TRANSITIONS – the way in which the shots move from one into the other producing a particular effect. Different transitions include cuts which produce a faster paced sequence. Fades and wipes suggest a more controlled and slower section.

USER – another term for a type of audience and suggests that this audience is active and involved in the media text in some way. Some media texts, for example websites and computer games, encourage interactivity.

UNIQUE SELLING POINT (USP) – the unique selling point of a media text is what will make the audience buy it! With reference to a CD cover, this may mean the artwork, the performer's motif or special features including previously unheard material or special guests.

VISUAL CODES – the clues in the text to help the audience analyse and understand it. Visual codes are split into:

Code of clothing – what is worn says something about the character and makes them easier to understand, for example uniforms, followers of football teams and bands, etc.

Code of expression – facial expressions give clues to emotions, for example a smile, a frown, etc.

Code of gesture – the way that bodies are moved communicates messages, for example a wave, thumbs up.

Code of technique – this is specific to media texts and is about the way in which the image is presented, for example the use of black and white suggests sophistication, the use of soft focus suggests romance, etc.

WATER COOLER TELEVISION – an American term which appeared in Britain at about the same time as the first series of *Big Brother*. It describes an immediate audience response whereby the next morning, around the water cooler; people are talking about what happened in a particular programme the night before.

WINDOW ON THE WORLD – the suggestion that news programmes and documentaries offer a realistic representation of what is going on in the world.

ZOO FORMAT – a style of radio programme where there is a main presenter but also others who contribute. The mode of address is informal and there are jokes and chat between the participants.

Quickfire answers

Quickfire 1

Other types of camera shot include:

A point of view shot – this is where the camera becomes the eyes of a character in the text and the audience then see the action from that character's perspective. This makes the audience feel involved with that character and what is happening but it may also be an uncomfortable position if, for example, you become the eyes of a stalker following their victim.

An extreme long shot – this is used to show space and may be, for example, the shot of the polar ice caps in a nature programme to emphasise the expanse and isolation of the location.

A cutaway shot – this is a shot of something other than the subject. For example, a presenter in a documentary may be on location in an inner city housing estate talking to camera about social deprivation. The camera may 'cutaway' to show a shot of youths gathered on a street corner. The purpose of this shot is to exemplify what the presenter is saying.

An over the shoulder shot – this is often used in an interview situation to focus upon the person who is speaking.

A two shot – a shot where two people are in the frame together, usually at the same level. This may be used in, for example, a chat show where a guest is being interviewed by a celebrity host.

Quickfire 2

Using your own examples comment on:

- Colour connotations, for example dark blues and purples, to suggest an evening fragrance in an advertisement.
- Font style giving clues to the genre of the text.
- The type of shot which can convey meaning – a close-up used on a film poster can give clues to the character and their role in the film.
- Effects employed, for example use of black and white to suggest sophistication, or airbrushing to give an effect of perfection.
- Choice of images.

Quickfire 3

Another example of a text that uses subject-specific lexis is a forensic crime drama, for example *Waking the Dead* or *CSI: Miami*. Here the language used is specifically related to scene of the crime evidence and forensic procedures. This makes the programme seem more realistic. The audience expect to hear this language and if they are regular watchers, begin to feel knowledgeable in this field and tend not to question the validity of the lexis used.

Quickfire 4

An informal mode of address makes the audience feel more relaxed and involved in the media text. Texts like teenage magazines will often use personal pronouns and a chatty tone to make their readers feel involved in the community of the magazine. Location news reporters from war zones, for example, will adopt a more formal mode of address through their expression, language and gestures to reflect the seriousness of the subject matter. The audience will then take what they are reporting seriously and trust their information.

Quickfire 5

In a good answer you would have chosen an appropriate text and discussed:

- Narrative and plot situations
- Technical and audio codes
- Settings and iconography
- Characters and representations.

You would have been able to demonstrate, through the repertoire of elements, how far your text is typical of its genre. You would have backed up your points with specific examples from your chosen text.

Quickfire 6

An image without words is open to the interpretation of the audience and will therefore differ according to the way in which an audience may decode the image. Once the producers of the text accompany the image with words, then they 'close down' the meaning of the image and the audience is much less likely to suggest an alternative meaning. They will accept the dominant or preferred reading. For example, if a photograph of Cheryl Cole appears on the front of a newspaper and the caption is 'devastated!' then the meaning is made clear. Exactly the same image may have the caption 'hopeful' and the meaning is completely changed.

Quickfire 7

A good answer should include an appropriate example and include an analysis of:

- Masthead
- Font style suggesting genre
- House style
- Cover lines
- Sell lines
- Discourse
- Central image
- Mode of address
- Other visual codes.

Reference must be made of the purpose and effect of the techniques employed.

Quickfire 8

Firstly, the purpose of the advertisement is different from that of advertisements for consumable products – this is not something we can actually buy. The aim of charity campaigns like this one is to raise our awareness and in this case, persuade us to give items to charity shops. The image of the small child is emotive; he is engaging directly with us and looks vulnerable. This is supported by the text which asks us to 'fight for a child's future'. We are encouraged to sympathise with his plight and we are made to feel that we can help in some way – he becomes the iconic representation the audience must 'buy into' rather than a consumable product.

Quickfire 9

Using an appropriate example you should have included some of the following in your answer:

- Endorsement
- Use of images
- Slogan
- Persuasive language and mode of address
- Layout and design
- Colour codes
- Appeal
- Typography and graphics
- Technical codes and intertextuality.

You must also discuss the purpose and effect of the techniques used in attracting the audience.

Quickfire 10

The genre of a film and its stars are two important ways in which a film is marketed to its audience. Giving clear indications of the film's genre in the marketing materials will attract fans of that genre, giving them indications of what to expect. The genre will be made clear on film posters and in trailers by the use of visual codes, music, narrative and characters. Stars are also key to selling a film and to giving an indication of the production values. If someone like, for example Liam Neeson, is in the film then he will show that the film is high budget but he will also attract his own fan base as well as an audience who are aware of the genre of film in which he tends to appear.

Quickfire 11 and 12

Web pages offer different opportunities and experiences to users than the print-based version. They allow the user to be interactive – they can take part in blogs, email the publication directly and have a certain amount of autonomy in choosing what aspects of the website they want to use. They can concentrate on certain parts and ignore others entirely. They can have access to multimedia features that are not available in the print version, for example videos, podcasts, music and animations. External web links can also guide the user to other related sites; this allows for a broader experience.

Quickfire 13

This front page can be used as an example for other areas of the MS1 paper, for example audience. Here you should have discussed who the primary and secondary audiences of the text may be. Also, how different audiences may respond to the text and for what reasons, for example age, cultural experience, etc. The text can also be used to discuss the representation of young people and an event in the media today – here you would need to consider the construction, language and mode of address of the text.

Quickfire 14

The news values may include:

- Threshold – this is a big story covered by all the papers that day.
- Negativity – it is bad news involving violence.
- Unexpectedness – the turn this event took was unexpected.
- Seemingly unambiguous – the image effectively and dramatically anchors the story.

Quickfire 15

Using specific examples you should have mentioned the following in your answer:

- A central image and title giving a clue to the genre of the game
- Recognisable characters presented through visual codes
- A sense of the narrative communicated through the plot synopsis and the thumbnail images
- A slogan and tag line
- Suggestions of setting
- Lexis related to the game play
- Links to other games produced suggesting quality and playing on audience expectations.

Quickfire 16

The Chris Moyles Show constructs a representation of men as 'laddish' through the mode of address, use of humour, content of the discussions as part of the zoo format and the fact that the programme and the presenter are often controversial. Chris Moyles has a reputation for this sort of behaviour and seems to enjoy being the subject of controversy. This could be linked to the ideology of this radio station, its scheduling and it target audience.

Quickfire 17

Using your own examples and remembering to discuss purpose and effect, you should have mentioned:

- The title of the film and connotations of this
- Genre codes and conventions
- The stars and audience expectations
- Technical codes and editing to maintain interest
- Audio codes suggesting genre
- Promises of pleasure
- Enigma codes
- Suggestions of quality including the director and/or previous films.

Quickfire 18

Your analysis of the still from *Waking the Dead* should cover some of the following points:

- The image suggests that the programme focuses around a team of men and women.
- The women are represented strongly through their direct mode of address and their code of gesture and expression.
- There is also a positive representation of an older woman who is smiling.
- The older man is at the front of the group and his code of clothing is more formal, suggesting a hierarchy with him in charge.
- The lighting is low key and there is no natural light, suggesting the tone and genre of the programme is metaphorically 'dark'.
- The iconography suggests the sub-genre of forensic crime drama: the setting is a lab/post-mortem room with sink and an examination table. The setting is also very sterile and clinical looking.
- The characters are not wearing white coats, suggesting they may have different roles within the drama.

Quickfire 19

The images show the following conventions of performance music videos:

- Shots of performers playing instruments to illustrate that they are 'real' musicians.
- The band performing in interesting locations (on a roof top) and then lip-synching.
- The performance as an 'event' showcasing individuals in the band, for example Gary Barlow.
- The use of close-up shots with a direct mode of address.
- The use of a motif that distinguishes the performer, for example Lady Gaga and her different persona in this video.

Quickfire 20

- It may affect the sense that the audience makes of the world.
- The representation contained within the text shapes the idea of what is 'normal', for example body shape.
- The representation may affect the audience response. For example, the audience may accept the preferred reading of the text or may challenge the representations as they are presented in the text.

Quickfire 21

The dominant ideology of a media text will be reflected through the way in which the text is constructed, the language, use of images and mode of address. For example, the *Daily Mail* usually constructs a negative view of young people and blames them for a lot of the problems in society. This was illustrated by their coverage of the August riots whereby they ran emotive headlines and dramatic images of young people. The readership of this paper has expectations of the view it will take and they will therefore accept the representation constructed by the text.

Quickfire 22

If the opinion leaders are trusted by the audience then they will accept their view of an event without question and will not seek to find further information first hand or from another source. This is particularly true if the opinion leader, for example a national newspaper, reaffirms what the reader thought in the first place, neither of which may be an unbiased view of the event.

Quickfire 23

- By buying the souvenir issues in recognition that this is an important event that will be important in the future.
- Feeling proud to be British and to be part of the event.
- By accepting the dominant reading that everyone should recognise this as an important event.
- Buying the papers to get the extra information and to be informed about the inside gossip and 'untold stories'.
- By feeling good as instructed by the *Daily Star*.

Quickfire 24

A good answer would use specific examples to illustrate how images, language, visual codes and mode of address construct the representation of an issue.

Quickfire 25

A good answer will use specific examples of texts to consider positive and negative representations of ethnicity in the music industry and to consider both the context and how the representation is constructed. This answer may cover positive representations that focus on cultural identity and negative examples of stereotypical representations of violence, difference and gang culture.

Quickfire 26

A good answer would select appropriate texts from those you have studied in class and comment on how the gender and/or age of the audience may affect the way in which they respond to that text. You may have considered the way in which the text is constructed including: narrative, themes, characters, technical and audio codes. You should also have discussed the different responses making reference to Hall's response theory of preferred, negotiated and oppositional. You must have referred to specific examples from your texts in your answer.

Quickfire 27

A good answer would have chosen an appropriate text studied in class and used specific examples from the text to illustrate the uses and gratifications theory. A good answer would also have avoided downloading theory without reference to examples.

Quickfire 28

The preferred reading of *Cosmopolitan* magazine will be from women who aspire to live the lifestyle constructed by the magazine. They will accept the ideology behind the magazine and its suggestions about what a 'normal' woman is in terms of body size and image, career and relationships.

The negotiated reading will be from 'pick and mix' readers who may not engage with overly sexual cover lines and content, as that does not attract them, but they may be interested in keeping up to date with the latest fashion and beauty advice provided by the magazine. They may then adapt this to suit their lives, understanding that Cosmopolitan Woman is a construct.

An oppositional reading may be from older women who see nothing in the magazine to attract them and object to and challenge the notions of lifestyle presented in the magazine.

Quickfire 29

- Mainstreamers may stick with the brands they have always bought as they trust them, for example Heinz and Kellogg's instead of supermarket brands.
- Aspirers are happy to buy products they can't really afford in order to make an impression. They are happy to pay on credit for the newest model of car or to buy a Prada handbag to demonstrate the status they wish they had in society.
- Succeeders have already achieved a particular high status and want to maintain it. They will be 'silver surfers'. They will always buy a Mercedes because it illustrates their social status, they have always driven one and found them reliable.
- Reformers want to think they can make a difference so they may buy FairTrade or organic products or be persuaded to donate to charities as a result of a campaign.

Quickfire 30

A good answer to this question would choose appropriate texts that allow you to discuss the key areas of audience including different responses, attraction and appeal and positioning.

ANALYSING TECHNICAL AND AUDIO CODES

TEXT:	CAMERA SHOTS/ANGLES	CAMERA MOVEMENT	EDITING TECHNIQUES	AUDIO CODES
EXAMPLES				
PURPOSE AND EFFECT				

ANALYSING PRINT TEXTS

TEXT:	LAYOUT AND DESIGN	VISUAL CODES	GENRE	LANGUAGE AND MODE OF ADDRESS
EXAMPLES				
PURPOSE AND EFFECT				

To be completed by the candidate
Pre-production
Production (including details of your contribution to group work, where relevant)
Report

NOTICE TO CANDIDATE
The work you submit for assessment must be your own.

If you copy from someone else, allow another candidate to copy from you, or if you cheat in any other way, including plagiarising material, you may be disqualified from at least the subject concerned.

Declaration by Candidate

I have read and understood the **Notice to Candidate** (above). I have produced the attached work without assistance other than that which my teacher has explained is acceptable within the specification.

Signature   Date

This form *must* be completed by all candidates and *must* accompany work submitted for moderation.

Index